Bodda Getta

Auburn's Remarkable Run

Presented by

OPELIKA-AUBURN
NEWS

Foreword

*"*G*ames like these come along only once in a long while. A team and its coach prove themselves great on the inside where the heart is. The public watches, understands, and is proud ..."*

Those words were written a long time ago—57 years ago in fact—by Jerry Bryan, a sportswriter for The Birmingham News, to describe another Auburn team at another place in time. Auburn trailed Mississippi State at Starkville 21-0 at the start of the fourth quarter. Shug Jordan's Tigers reached deep within and found the specialness they needed to come back and tie – Auburn people always considered it a "win" since this was before the days of the two-point extra point – 21-21.

Those same words could have been written again this year, 2010, many times over and of the team and the season as a whole: "Teams like this come along only once in a long while. A team and its coach prove themselves great on the inside where the heart is. The public watches, understands, and is proud ..."

Ladies and Gentlemen, the 2010 Auburn Tigers.

Time and time again they were down, sometimes by two touchdowns or more, but they were never out. Their spirit, their desire, their

confidence, their belief in one another, their belief in "work, hard work," as defined in the Auburn Creed, and their absolute refusal to give up made this team special and enabled it to become one of the greatest Auburn teams of all time.

And there it shall remain, for as long as football is played in this place called Auburn, and for as long as Auburn sunsets are orange and blue.

There are many things that can and should be said about this team. Other undefeated Auburn teams may have had more talent, but no Auburn team has exceeded this one in heart, soul, courage, unity and oneness. Perhaps these words about another team of long ago say it best: "They believed in themselves, their destiny they knew, and they had the stuff to make their dreams come true..."

And by making their dream come true, by having a season no one could have predicted and a season perhaps they themselves never expected or anticipated, they have given Auburn people many Saturdays to remember, memories and moments that will last a lifetime. When the fans of the 2010 team are old and gray, when they are sitting around the fireside with their grandchildren on their knees, they will still be talking about the Auburn Tigers of 2010.

It won't be so much about the games won as it will be about the way they played the game, with heart, enthusiasm, courage, commitment and contagious joy, a joy best captured by the smile of Cam Newton, one of many heroes on this very special team. "Yes, we Cam..." Yes, they could, and yes, they did. That they won made it all the better. They will be remembered forever.

As they should be.

David Housel

David Housel
Historian and Lifelong Auburn Man

Table of Contents

Note: Home team is listed first. Weekly Associated Press rankings were used for this publication.

September 4, 2010 • Auburn, Alabama • W 52-26

Newton makes himself at home in Auburn debut

Andrew Gribble | Staff Writer

Cameron Newton dropped back in the pocket, spun out of one tackle and stared another Arkansas State defender in the face during one of the most important moments in the second quarter of Saturday's game.

Spin, wiggle, slap, shimmy, break.

Newton was finally in the open field, dashing to the opposite sideline for a 16-yard gain. Two plays later, he plunged into the end zone from 2 yards out, the second of his five touchdowns.

This was what Auburn fans had been anxiously waiting for from the dynamic junior-college transfer, who broke out in a big way Saturday in the Tigers' 52-26 season-opening victory over Arkansas State.

"I'm just blessed to be in this situation," Newton said, "and be able to make plays when I can make plays."

His 171 rushing yards on just 15 carries set an Auburn single-game record for the most by a quarterback, snapping a 36-year-old record held by Phil Gargis. He completed nine of his 14 passes for 186 yards and three touchdowns, hitting Mario Fannin twice from 36 and 38 yards, and Quindarius Carr from 48.

"It's really big but it's on to the next one," Newton said. "Of course, I'm happy with the accolade but I feel I didn't play the best game I could play."

His highlight-reel maneuvers for that 16-yard gain were by far the toughest yards he amassed all night. The rest of his 357 yards of total offense looked effortless against an overmatched Arkansas State defense.

"As the game went on, I felt my feet settling in," said Newton, whose night was over after Auburn scored its seventh and final touchdown early in the fourth quarter.

"When it was time for me to make plays, I was able to make plays."

These were plays Newton wasn't able to show his teammates and coaches in camp since he arrived on campus in January. At the moment he stepped onto Auburn's practice field for the first spring practice, Newton was cloaked in an orange, non-contact jersey, inhibiting his ability to make plays on the fly and, particularly, with his feet.

Coach Gene Chizik was just like the 83,441 in attendance. He had no idea what to expect, yet left excited about Newton's potential in games that matter a little more than Saturday's.

"He did some nice things when maybe something wasn't there," Chizik said. "He turned bad plays into potentially good ones."

His first big run came at a surprisingly critical time, when Auburn, already down 6-0, faced a third-and-long midway through the first quarter. With no one open, Newton sprinted up the middle and juked two linebackers before diving 1 yard in front of the chains for a first down.

Three plays later, Auburn was in the end zone, helped by a 36-yard run from Onterio McCalebb and capped with a Kodi Burns 3-yard dive, and never trailed again.

OPPOSITE: Cam Newton (2) takes off on a sneak as Byron Isom (57) looks to make a block during Auburn's season opener against Arkansas State at Jordan-Hare Stadium in Auburn. VASHA HUNT/OPELIKA-AUBURN NEWS

BELOW: Coach Gene Chizik works the crowd. VASHA HUNT/OPELIKA-AUBURN NEWS

But it was just the beginning to Newton's breakout showcase.

He followed by leading Auburn to touchdowns on four of the next five drives, helping the Tigers' proficient offense overcome a troubling display from their pass defense, which surrendered 323 yards.

None of the possessions lasted longer than four plays, or one minute and 26 seconds. He capped the second-quarter display with a 71-yard touchdown run off a broken play, one in which he awkwardly faked a handoff to McCalebb, raced up the middle untouched and sprinted past everyone in sight with yards to burn.

"Cam's got some big legs and calf muscles," said freshman Michael Dyer, who had quite the impressive debut, himself, finishing with 95 rushing yards and a touchdown.

"He's 6-6. That's a grown man you're talking about."

Newton wasn't perfect. He overthrew a couple of open receivers on crossing patterns and even launched a throw to the sidelines on a simple screen pass. He also looked clumsy at times when he thought his feet were the ticket out of trouble when, in fact, they just made for a bigger loss of yards.

These plays certainly didn't escape the eyes of offensive coordinator Gus Malzahn, who was already burning mad about poor clock management late in the second quarter, three fumbles (two lost) within the span of five minutes in the third quarter and seven penalties, the majority of which were committed by his players.

Yet even Malzahn, Auburn's No. 1 perfectionist, left impressed by what Newton did both through the air and with his feet.

"I think it changes the way defenses play you," Malzahn said. "You've got to be aware, because he's got some big-play ability that can make things (happen) when a play breaks down." ∎

ABOVE: Auburn's Mike Blanc (93) blocks an extra point. VASHA HUNT/OPELIKA-AUBURN NEWS

RIGHT: Auburn's Darvin Adams has the ball knocked away by ASU's Walter Moody. VASHA HUNT/OPELIKA-AUBURN NEWS

OPPOSITE LEFT: Auburn running back Onterio McCalebb gets loose. VASHA HUNT/OPELIKA-AUBURN NEWS

OPPOSITE RIGHT ABOVE: The sun sets on Jordan-Hare during a TV timeout. VASHA HUNT/OPELIKA-AUBURN NEWS

OPPOSITE RIGHT BELOW: Darvin Adams hauls in an over-the-shoulder catch to get the ball to the 1-yard line. VASHA HUNT/OPELIKA-AUBURN NEWS

Mississippi State vs. ²¹Auburn

September 9, 2010 • Starkville, Mississippi • W 17-14

Auburn defense shuts down Mississippi State

Andrew Gribble | Staff Writer

STARKVILLE, Miss. — Auburn left Davis Wade Stadium on Thursday night wounded and probably a little deafened.

It just didn't leave defeated.

There's something about Mississippi State's stadium and its cowbell-ringing fans that brings some ugly out of Auburn's offense. But the Tigers, aided by a hard-nosed defensive effort, escaped with yet another SEC-opening victory, 17-14.

"It won't be perfect when we look at it tomorrow," coach Gene Chizik said. "But it was good enough."

The much-maligned Auburn defense made stop after stop in Thursday's second half, limiting the Bulldogs' offense, which racked up 569 yards in its season opener, to just 73 yards on the game's final five drives. At one point, while Auburn's offense sputtered and stalled in an unfamiliar fashion, the unit forced three consecutive three-and-outs, looking nothing like the defense that surrendered 323 passing yards and 26 points to Arkansas State in the season opener.

Mississippi State finished with 246 yards of offense.

"There are a lot of experts out there," defensive coordinator Ted Roof said of the perception that Thursday night's game would be an offensive shootout.

"I was really proud of how hard they fought together and hung together. It wasn't always pretty, but to hold them to 240 yards, I'm really proud of that."

Auburn might not have always been in the right spot on Mississippi State's final possession, but it combined a relentless pass rush with a little bit of luck to ultimately send the Bulldogs to their 11th consecutive SEC-opening loss.

Taking over on its own 20-yard line, Mississippi State converted a key fourth down on a 21-yard pass from Chris Relf to Arceto Clark. Following a crushing sack from Nick Fairley, Mississippi State picked up another big first down on a third-and-long incompletion that ended with a pass interference flag on T'Sharvan Bell.

Another first down, and the Bulldogs would have been in kicker Sean Brauchle's comfort zone.

"We didn't let that get to us," Fairley said. "We got right back out there."

Josh Bynes applied heavy pressure on Relf to force an incompletion on first down. On second down, Relf had cornerback Neiko Thorpe completely turned around and zipped a crisp pass into the hands of Leon Berry 20 yards down the field.

Berry, though, dropped the ball.

"The opportunity was there for us to win," said Bulldogs coach Dan Mullen, who added that Bulldogs' receivers dropped five passes that hit their hands.

"We need to do that for this program to turn the corner."

Relf's final two passes were way off. His game-ender sailed out of bounds and in the direction of no one in particular as a result of miscommunication between he and Berry.

"Those kids fought through that penalty on that last drive," Roof said. "That's a sign of growth."

Cameron Newton's growth was on display in his first game against SEC competition, as he demonstrated that the skills he showed in carving up Arkansas State do translate to the next level.

He carried the Auburn offense once again, throwing for 136 yards and two touchdowns and rushing for a team-best 70, a number of which were gained on key sneaks for first downs.

The effort just wasn't as spotless as his debut, as the Tigers' offense only seemed to click on their two drives that ended in touchdowns in the first half. Newton hit Emory Blake on a short screen that ended as a 39-yard touchdown reception on the game's opening drive and then connected with Darvin Adams for a 13-yard touchdown pass midway through the second quarter.

One week after rolling to the tune of 608 yards of offense, Auburn finished with 348 on Thursday. Auburn

---

OPPOSITE: Auburn's defense swarms Mississippi State running back Vick Ballard (28) during the second half of the Auburn-Mississippi State game in Starkville, Miss. Auburn won a squeaker 17-14.
VASHA HUNT/OPELIKA-AUBURN NEWS

BELOW: Auburn defensive back Aairon Savage (2) takes down MSU's Chris Smith (8). VASHA HUNT/OPELIKA-AUBURN NEWS

gained just 133 yards in its scoreless second half, its first half without points since last year's Oct. 17 loss to Kentucky.

"We're going to have to play much better offense," Chizik said. "We did sustain some drives to eat some clock."

The win didn't come without a few key losses to Auburn's offense. Offensive tackle Lee Ziemba, a preseason All-SEC first-team selection, exited with an apparent knee injury and did not return. Tailback Mario Fannin injured his shoulder early in the fourth quarter on a rough collision and also did not return.

Both players will be re-evaluated today.

"It was a team win," Chizik said, "and some guys had to step up to the plate."

Those guys were members of Auburn's defense.

"We had to man up and see where we are," Fairley said. "It was an SEC win on the road and that is good for us." ∎

RIGHT: Auburn wide receiver Terrell Zachery (81) looks for running room. VASHA HUNT/OPELIKA-AUBURN NEWS

BELOW: Auburn defensive back Neiko Thorpe (15) lines up during the first half. VASHA HUNT/OPELIKA-AUBURN NEWS

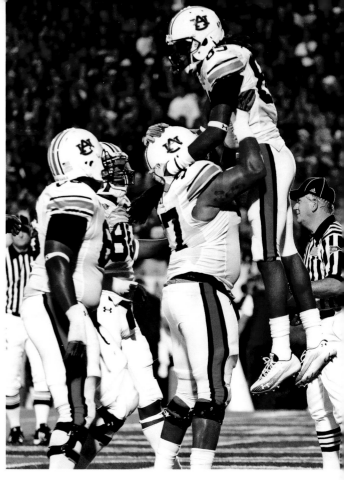

ABOVE: Auburn offensive lineman A.J. Greene (77) gives Auburn wide receiver Darvin Adams (89) a boost as they celebrate the Tiger's second touchdown during the first half. VASHA HUNT/OPELIKA-AUBURN NEWS

LEFT ABOVE: Auburn players signal a fumble recovery during the first half. VASHA HUNT/OPELIKA-AUBURN NEWS

LEFT: Auburn's Demond Washington (14) returns a punt upfield as Craig Sanders (13) makes a block. VASHA HUNT/OPELIKA-AUBURN NEWS

ABOVE: Mississippi State wide receiver Brandon Heavens drops a pass that was in his hands with under a minute to play in the second half. VASHA HUNT/OPELIKA-AUBURN NEWS

BELOW: Auburn long snapper Josh Harris (61) chest bumps a cheerleader. VASHA HUNT/OPELIKA-AUBURN NEWS

ABOVE: Auburn defensive back Neiko Thorpe tips a pass away from Mississippi State's Arceto Clark during the second half. VASHA HUNT/OPELIKA-AUBURN NEWS

OPPOSITE: Mississippi State's Johnthan Banks loses his helmet as he tackles Auburn's Demond Washington during a return in the first half. VASHA HUNT/OPELIKA-AUBURN NEWS

September 18, 2010 • Auburn, Alabama • W 27-24 OT

Auburn survives overtime scare

Andrew Gribble | Staff Writer

Athletics director Jay Jacobs was one of the first to storm the field, ready to give anyone in sight two leaping high fives.

Sophomore cornerback T'Sharvan Bell had his arm wrapped around two Navy soldiers, shimmying back and forth as cheers of "SEC! SEC!" echoed throughout the Tigers' student section.

The 87,451 fans, many of whom started their day at 8 a.m. by holding signs behind ESPN's GameDay stage, were waving their "True Blue" pompoms long after Clemson kicker Chandler Catanzaro's 32-yard field goal attempt sailed wide left, sending Auburn to an improbable, 27-24 overtime victory.

This non-conference victory meant as much on paper as Auburn's season-opening snoozer of a win against Arkansas State, but you sure could have fooled the players, coaches and fans who streamed out of Jordan-Hare Stadium on Saturday night.

"They kept their faith the whole game, and it was one of those games where they just kept fighting," coach Gene Chizik said. "We can win games when we play with a lot of heart. We can win games when we play with a lot of faith."

That faith was tested in so many ways Saturday, but none more so than the Tigers' final defensive stand.

Leading by 3 following Wes Byrum's 39-yard field goal on the first possession of overtime, Auburn gave up a quick first down on an 8-yard screen pass from Kyle Parker to Andre Ellington. This was a running theme throughout an up-and-down night for the Tigers' defense, which largely let Parker undress it with short passes to his running backs and tight ends all night.

An Ellington rush for 5 yards set up a short second down, but a Zac Etheridge tackle in Clemson's back-field, followed by a dropped Parker pass in the end zone set up Clemson for a game-tying, 27-yard field goal.

Catanzaro made it with no sweat, booting the ball straight down the middle to apparently send the game to a second overtime. But penalty flags laid on both sides of the field, prompting officials to huddle away from overzealous players and coaches on both sides of the field.

Someone moved. It was just a matter of figuring out who did and what exactly caused it.

Clemson coach Dabo Swinney said he was originally told that an Auburn defender jumped offsides, a call that would have put Clemson on Auburn's 3-yard line with a first-and-goal. He soon found out that his long snapper, Matt Skinner, committed an illegal snap, which, by rule, unfairly drew the defenders offsides.

"It's awful tough to see points come off the scoreboard like that," Swinney said. "That's football."

Those points never came back.

LEFT: ESPN's "College GameDay" broadcasts from the Auburn campus early on the day of the Auburn-Clemson game.
VASHA HUNT/OPELIKA-AUBURN NEWS

OPPOSITE: Cam Newton (2) runs to the sidelines celebrating after Auburn's overtime win. Auburn won 27-24 on Clemson's missed field goal.
VASHA HUNT/OPELIKA-AUBURN NEWS

By the time Catanzaro's kick sailed wide, Pat Dye Field was covered by jubilant Auburn players.

"I think that is part of them just staying in there and hanging in and fighting and clawing and scratching until they find a way to win it," Chizik said. "I couldn't be more proud of just the way they responded."

The response Auburn mustered in the third quarter was what put the Tigers in their fortunate position at the end.

Auburn managed just 8 yards of offense in the first quarter and didn't pick up a first down until its fourth offensive series. Meanwhile, Clemson controlled possession in dominating fashion, holding the ball for 19 of the game's first 22 minutes.

Parker's 24-yard pass to Jamie Harper with 1:14 to play in the second quarter put Clemson up, 17-0, and elicited a few, sparse boos. Auburn prevented a four-quarter scoreless streak, dating back to a scoreless second half at Mississippi State last week, by its quick, 2-minute drill response, an effort that ended with a 35-yard Byrum field goal to make it 17-3.

"We just needed to put points on the board," offensive coordinator Gus Malzahn said. "That gave us a good feeling going into the second half."

Auburn's offense was simply electric in the third quarter, as quarterback Cameron Newton led the

Tigers down the field on four consecutive possessions. His second interception of the night stymied the first drive, but the next three ended with touchdowns. His 78-yard pump-fake deep ball to Terrell Zachery near the end of the third quarter gave Auburn its first lead and capped a run of 24 unanswered points.

The Tigers gained 116 yards in the first half only to gain 258 in the third quarter alone.

"It was really nothing but chalk flying at halftime on a bunch of adjustments," Chizik said.

Auburn's defense, shredded and exposed by a Clemson offense that was "very vanilla" in its first two games this season, bent frequently through the second half, but only broke once. Parker responded immediately after Zachery's touchdown, leading Clemson on a nine-play, 75-yard drive, which was capped with a 2-yard, game-tying touchdown run by Ellington.

In a position to win the game in regulation, Clemson drove to its own 48-yard line with less than 3 minutes to play, but couldn't convert a key third-down play.

Auburn took over inside its own 20 with 1:23 to play. The high-risk, high-reward offense opted to play it safe and take the game into overtime.

"We just want to make it exciting," Chizik said. "That's for sure." ∎

LEFT: Cam Newton (2) throws an interception during the first half, which was dominated by Clemson. VASHA HUNT/OPELIKA-AUBURN NEWS

OPPOSITE LEFT BELOW: Cam Newton high-fives fans during TigerWalk. VASHA HUNT/OPELIKA-AUBURN NEWS

OPPOSITE RIGHT ABOVE: Fans cheer for Auburn as ESPN shoots in 3D during pre-game festivities. VASHA HUNT/OPELIKA-AUBURN NEWS

OPPOSITE RIGHT MIDDLE: War Eagle VII, Nova, touches down before the game. VASHA HUNT/OPELIKA-AUBURN NEWS

OPPOSITE RIGHT BELOW: Fans cheer at the start of the game. VASHA HUNT/OPELIKA-AUBURN NEWS

ABOVE: Auburn's Onterio McCalebb tries to break through the line during the first half.
VASHA HUNT/OPELIKA-AUBURN NEWS

RIGHT: Auburn wide receiver Terrell Zachery catches a pass from Cam Newton then tip-toes along the sideline before running the ball in for a 78-yard touchdown. VASHA HUNT/OPELIKA-AUBURN NEWS

BELOW: Auburn running back Michael Dyer (5) gets loose. VASHA HUNT/OPELIKA-AUBURN NEWS

LEFT: Trooper Taylor revs up the team during the second half. VASHA HUNT/OPELIKA-AUBURN NEWS

FAR LEFT: Auburn defensive back Demond Washington breaks up a pass to Clemson's Jamie Harper. VASHA HUNT/OPELIKA-AUBURN NEWS

BELOW: Auburn safety Zac Etheridge (4), quarterback Cam Newton (2) and running back Michael Dyer (5) get the fans pumped up at the beginning of the overtime period.
VASHA HUNT/OPELIKA-AUBURN NEWS

back Demond Washington. "It paid off in the end."

Though Auburn's offense scored three unanswered touchdowns in the third period, the AU defense responded with a big quarter itself — allowing Clemson just 46 yards — as the Tigers turned a 17-3 deficit into a 24-17 lead.

Auburn did not force any turnovers, but rattled Clemson quarterback Kyle Parker in the second half. The two-sport star completed just 5-of-11 passes in the second half for 33 yards after burning Auburn for 227 yards in the first half.

Clemson had 267 total yards at the half – and only 127 the rest of the game.

"There was nothing but chalk flying at halftime with a bunch of adjustments," Auburn head coach Gene Chizik explained. "So we kind of had to see what their game plan was. They caught our offense off guard early with some things they were doing." ∎

ABOVE: Clemson place kicker Chandler Cantanzaro misses the potential game-tying field goal in overtime to give Auburn the victory. VASHA HUNT/OPELIKA-AUBURN NEWS

OPPOSITE: Auburn fan and Tigerette Host Emily Jenkins screams for the Tigers during the overtime period. VASHA HUNT/OPELIKA-AUBURN NEWS

BELOW: Fans celebrate. VASHA HUNT/OPELIKA-AUBURN NEWS

Defense makes the stop

Joe McAdory | Staff Writer

Eight yards away from defeat in the crunch of overtime, Auburn defenders dug deep. They'd already allowed Clemson 414 yards and stared down the barrel of their first defeat of the season.

"We knew that some how, some way, we had to come up with a stop," said senior linebacker Craig Stevens, playing his first game after a two-game suspension.

And that's what happened.

On second-and-5 from the Auburn 8, Clemson tailback Andre Ellington – who led all rushers with 140 yards – burst to the left with the first-down marker, goal line and victory in sight.

Instead, he was met hard by Neiko Thorpe and Zac Etheridge just before he could turn the corner. No gain. Third-and-5.

"In the fourth quarter, I almost gave up the game," said Etheridge, whose broken coverage on a fourth quarter Clemson pass play nearly led to a score. Instead, tight end Dwayne Allen dropped the pass. "In overtime, I had a chance to redeem myself."

With Ellington about to turn the corner at the 8, "I ran up and made the tackle," Etheridge said.

"We knew we had to get a big stop," said defensive

¹⁷Auburn vs. ¹²South Carolina

September 25, 2010 • Auburn, Alabama • W 35-27

Tigers force late turnovers to beat South Carolina

David Morrison | Staff Writer

South Carolina went to the well one too many times.

True freshman quarterback Connor Shaw, trying to lead a comeback in front of 87,237 screaming fans, lofted a pass in the corner of the end zone for Alshon Jeffery, who had shredded the Tigers' secondary all night for 192 yards on eight catches.

But Jeffery had company — three defensive backs' worth of it — and the ball glanced off his fingertips and into the waiting arms of junior Demond Washington.

The first interception by the Auburn secondary this season. The last of four South Carolina turnovers in the last 15 minutes.

The final blow in a 35-27 comeback win for the 17th-ranked Tigers over the 12th-ranked Gamecocks, one that keeps them perfect on the season and serves as the signature win of their first four games.

"Our guys have just responded," coach Gene Chizik said. "It is not always pretty. There are a lot of things as we look back on it are not good. These guys are fighting, clawing and scratching and trying to find a way to win every week."

Auburn's (4-0, 2-0 SEC) defense had managed only two turnovers over the season's 14 quarters before the floodgates opened in the second half.

The first came courtesy of Daren Bates, who jarred the ball loose from Gamecocks quarterback Stephen Garcia for T'Sharvan Bell to pick up.

The fumble came just after a missed 23-yard field goal from Wes Byrum that would have brought the

Tigers' deficit to 3. It ended with a 7-yard floater from Cameron Newton to Philip Lutzenkirchen on a play-action pass, putting the Tigers up 1 with 13:35 to go in the game.

Garcia drove the Gamecocks past midfield on their next drive, then coughed the ball up on a sack by Josh Bynes and Nosa Eguae, with Mike Blanc falling on it at the Auburn 47.

"We knew we had to play our game," Eguae said. "Up front we had to dominate. Coach (Tracy) Rocker said from the beginning if we dominate up front we are going to win this game."

Auburn made that hurt with Emory Blake's hurdling, high-stepping, tackle-breaking, 12-yard catch and run from Newton, putting the Tigers up 35-27 with 6:23 to go.

That's when South Carolina coach Steve Spurrier went to Shaw, who promptly drove the Gamecocks back down to the Auburn 25.

But he didn't see Bynes drop back into coverage on a first-down play, and the senior linebacker put hands to the Tigers' second interception of the season at their own 11 with 3:19 to go.

South Carolina (3-1, 1-1) forced a three-and-out —

OPPOSITE: Auburn linebacker Josh Bynes (17) and defensive back Daren Bates (25) celebrate a turnover during the Auburn-South Carolina game in Auburn. VASHA HUNT/OPELIKA-AUBURN NEWS

BELOW: Auburn defensive back Demond Washington makes the game-clinching interception. Auburn won 35-27 to down the higher-ranked USC Gamecocks. VASHA HUNT/OPELIKA-AUBURN NEWS

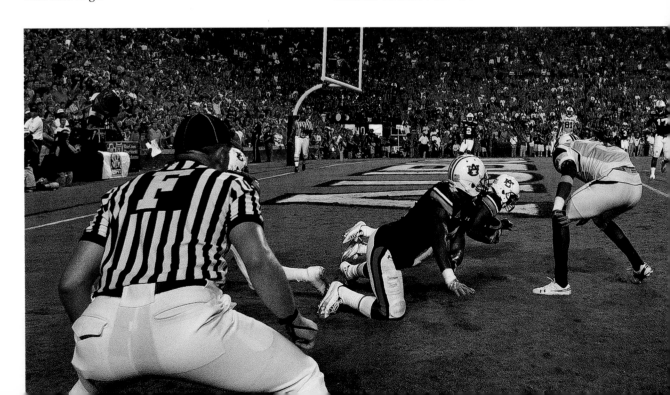

and the only Auburn punt of the second half — and had one more chance with 87 seconds on the clock.

Shaw went to Jeffery for 21 yards, then took it for 8 himself on a scramble to the AU 18.

The second time he looked Jeffery's way didn't turn out as well.

"My hat goes off to Neiko Thorpe and Zac (Etheridge) as they were there to make the play with me. I was just the one to make the play," Washington said. "But my hat really goes off to the entire defensive unit as a whole."

For the second week in a row, Auburn trailed at the break and still came back to win, this time against a ranked opponent.

And, for the second week in a row, a late score in the first half helped revive a struggling team.

The Tigers drove 76 yards on 12 plays, chewing up 5:30 and scoring on a 4-yard run by Newton.

Newton bounced back from his mini-slump in a big way, running for 176 yards and three scores on 25 carries and completing 16-of-21 passes for 158 yards and two touchdowns.

Auburn held the ball for 19:33 in the second half, running 49 plays to South Carolina's 22 and effectively putting a stranglehold on the game.

But it still took some late heroics from the defense.

"Coach Chizik was telling us all week that we needed to force more turnovers. We went out there and did that," Blanc said. "We have a great defensive line and a great secondary and we decided that we were not going to let us beat us." ∎

RIGHT ABOVE: Auburn players take the field.
VASHA HUNT/OPELIKA-AUBURN NEWS

RIGHT: Auburn quarterback Cam Newton (2) makes a cut to head upfield.
VASHA HUNT/OPELIKA-AUBURN NEWS

ABOVE: Auburn defensive lineman Nick Fairley pressures South Carolina quarterback Stephen Garcia. VASHA HUNT/OPELIKA-AUBURN NEWS

LEFT: Cam Newton smiles as he breaks a 54-yard touchdown run. VASHA HUNT/OPELIKA-AUBURN NEWS

BELOW: Auburn running back Onterio McCalebb (23) cuts to the outside. VASHA HUNT/OPELIKA-AUBURN NEWS

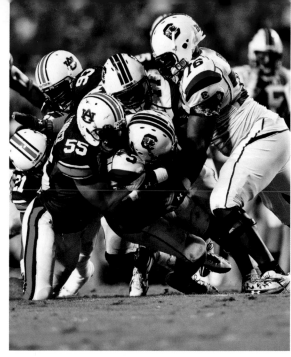

ABOVE: Auburn defensive end Corey Lemonier (55) sacks South Carolina quarterback Stephen Garcia (5). VASHA HUNT/OPELIKA-AUBURN NEWS

BELOW: Auburn quarterback Cam Newton (2) scores another touchdown. VASHA HUNT/OPELIKA-AUBURN NEWS

ABOVE: Cam Newton (2) celebrates his second touchdown of the night. VASHA HUNT/OPELIKA-AUBURN NEWS

OPPOSITE RIGHT ABOVE: Auburn running back Michael Dyer (5) works the fans before the game. VASHA HUNT/OPELIKA-AUBURN NEWS

OPPOSITE LEFT BELOW: Michael Dyer (5) get loose between the tackles. VASHA HUNT/OPELIKA-AUBURN NEWS

RIGHT: Auburn cheerleaders raise the Auburn flag following a touchdown. VASHA HUNT/OPELIKA-AUBURN NEWS

Auburn's Dyer bests fellow freshman phenom Lattimore

Joe McAdory | Staff Writer

Gene Chizik challenged Mike Dyer, and Auburn's freshman running back responded.

Dyer, rated by ESPN as the nation's No. 1 high school running back last year, rushed 23 times for 100 yards —67 more yards than South Carolina freshman Marcus Lattimore in the Tigers' 35-27 win Saturday night.

Lattimore, rated No. 2 by ESPN last year, chose South Carolina over Auburn on National Signing Day.

"I couldn't be more proud of a young guy," said Chizik, Auburn's second-year head coach. "I said

before the game, 'Are you ready to carry it 20 times?' He laughed and said, 'Are you kidding me?' He got stronger as the game went on."

Dyer rushed 15 times for 78 yards in the second half alone as Auburn erased a 20-14 deficit.

"Coach called the right plays at the right times," Dyer said. "Guys responded well and we did everything we were supposed to do tonight. In the second half, we went out there and did what was asked of us. Our offensive line just dominated in the second half. Whatever it took, however long it took, they came up and gave it their best. Sometimes we needed them so they responded. Whatever third downs or fourth downs we need, they came through. It would have never started without the line."

Dyer was part of a rushing rotation that burned the SEC's top-ranked rushing defense for 334 yards — including 187 in the second half. Coming in, No. 12 South Carolina (3-1) had held its opponents (Southern Miss, Georgia and Furman) to an average of 59.7 yards.

The Gamecocks received repeated doses of Dyer in the third and fourth quarters for gains of 6 to 8 yards as the Tigers kept moving the chains. Dyer did not

have a gain of more than 10 yards.

Through four games, Dyer has 62 attempts for 312 yards and a touchdown — leading all Auburn running backs. Sophomore Onterio McCalebb has 280 yards.

Quarterback Cameron Newton, who led all rushers with 176 yards with a game-high 25 attempts, doesn't mind sharing the ball with a freshman.

"He's producing," Newton said. "Giving him the ball that many times ... I know what he's capable of doing. If the line can give him that extra block, he's going to break it."

Dyer was temporarily yanked from the rotation late in the first period after fumbling — just one series after Mario Fannin coughed up the ball on a screen play.

"He had one mishap where he couldn't hold on to the ball," Chizik said. "That's nothing he can't fix. He'll learn from that." Dyer said Saturday's win was a trial by fire.

"Everybody in here is family," he said. "When family goes through trials, they stick together, and that is what this family did. We stick together no matter what we do. We had several fumbles, and the offensive line said keep going, we know you all are better than that."

■

RIGHT: Auburn defensive lineman Nick Fairley stares down South Carolina quarterback Stephen Garcia. VASHA HUNT/OPELIKA-AUBURN NEWS

FAR RIGHT: Auburn wide receiver Antonio Goodwin (6) acknowledges the crowd. VASHA HUNT/OPELIKA-AUBURN NEWS

BELOW: Auburn wide receiver Emory Blake (80) scores the final touchdown of the game on a pass reception. VASHA HUNT/OPELIKA-AUBURN NEWS

¹⁰Auburn vs. Louisiana-Monroe

October 2, 2010 • Auburn, Alabama • W 52-3

Auburn's kick-start offense pummels ULM

David Morrison | Staff Writer

Onterio McCalebb took a speed sweep around the right tackle on Auburn's second play from scrimmage, cut to the sideline and sprinted untouched to the end zone for a 50-yard score.

Not impressed?

The next time the Tigers got the ball — on their second play from scrimmage — Cameron Newton faked a draw into the line, stepped back and heaved a pass to hash marks, an open field and Emory Blake, who took it 94 yards for another score.

It was the longest play from scrimmage in Auburn history, edging Chris Todd's 93-yard touchdown pass to Terrell Zachery against Louisiana Tech in last year's opener.

"They saw the fake and they bit on it hard. There was no one there," Blake said. "I think it's a great honor just to be in the (record) books. It's probably going to get broken.

"But it's good to be in there for a little bit."

Auburn had a 14-point lead and used all of 74 seconds to do it. That was just the beginning in the Tigers' 52-3 win against Louisiana-Monroe in front of 80,759 fans at Jordan-Hare Stadium on Saturday.

The 10th-ranked Tigers (5-0) showed no signs of the slow starts that plagued them in comeback wins over Clemson and South Carolina, putting up 343 yards and 31 points on only 28 plays in the first half against ULM (1-3).

After a Radi Jabour 35-yard field goal cut Auburn's lead to 14-3, the Tigers came back with a Wes Byrum field goal, a 3-yard Mike Dyer run and a 16-yard pass from Newton to Quindarius Carr to take a 28-point lead into the break.

Newton, who ran 25 times against South Carolina, had only one official carry Saturday — an 11-yard sack right before halftime. He also completed 14-of-19 passes for 245 yards, three touchdowns and had a third-quarter interception.

"Our plan was to keep him from running too much," offensive coordinator Gus Malzahn said. "He's carried the ball a lot the last couple weeks. We'll do whatever

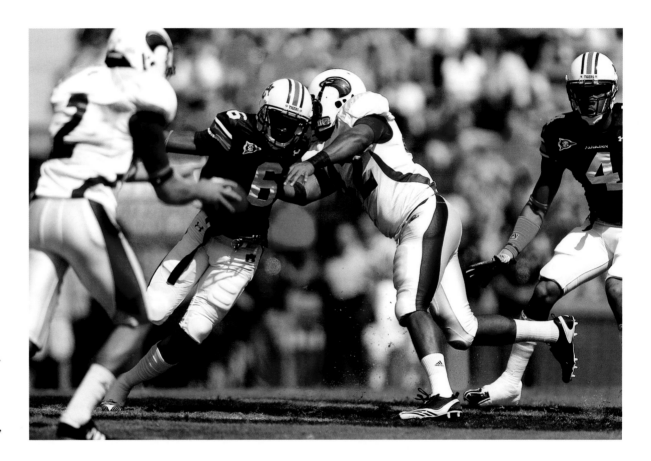

ABOVE: Auburn safety Jonathon Mincy (6) rushes the punter in a game with Louisiana-Monroe in Auburn. CLIFF WILLIAMS/OPELIKA-AUBURN NEWS

OPPOSITE: Emory Blake heads for paydirt after hauling in a pass for a 94-yard first-quarter touchdown reception. CLIFF WILLIAMS/OPELIKA-AUBURN NEWS

we have to do to win the game. Today, we didn't have to run."

That is, the Tigers didn't have to run with Newton.

Nine Auburn backs carried the ball 33 times for 233 yards — actually hurting the Tigers' SEC-leading average a smidge — with Mario Fannin's 10 rushes for 89 yards and a touchdown leading the way.

Fannin, who has been plagued by shoulder and fumble issues all season, had nine carries for 25 yards in Auburn's first four games.

The senior hadn't recorded double-digit carries in a game since running 13 times for 45 yards against UT-Martin on Nov. 8, 2008.

"I think his confidence is getting back up there with just getting nicked and beat up," coach Gene Chizik said. "It was good to see him run the ball like he did today."

The second half was for emptying the benches, as a total of 67 Auburn players saw action in the game, nine different receivers caught a pass and 31 different

Tigers recorded a tackle.

Barrett Trotter relieved Newton in the third quarter and led two scoring drives of his own, cashing in the second one himself on an 18-yard scramble that left the sophomore a bit shaken up.

And unlike the blowouts against Ball State and Furman last year, in which the second-team defense meant three or four scores for the opposition, the Tigers' backups held the Warhawks scoreless after the break.

"You can tell we're just getting better. The young guys are hungry," redshirt freshman defensive end Nosa Eguae said. "We all know when you get the chance, you better make plays, because chances are limited here."

For the first time in a month, and with a stretch of four SEC games coming up, Auburn got to relax in the fourth quarter.

"It was a bizarre feeling, very bizarre," Chizik said with a slight smirk. "But I will take it every time." ■

ABOVE: Auburn's Josh Bynes (17) lines up at linebacker and focuses in on the Louisana-Monroe offense. CLIFF WILLIAMS/OPELIKA-AUBURN NEWS

TOP: Fans cheer for Auburn. VASHA HUNT/OPELIKA-AUBURN NEWS

LEFT: Auburn quarterback Cam Newton revs up the crowd after passing for a 94-yard touchdown. VASHA HUNT/OPELIKA-AUBURN NEWS

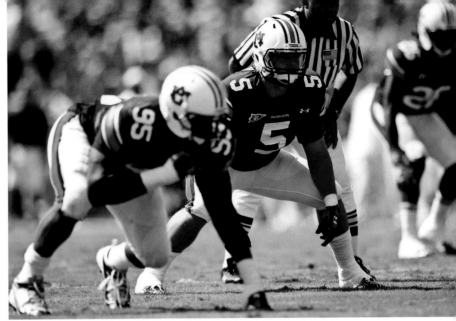

ABOVE: Auburn linebacker Jake Holland (5) sets up. VASHA HUNT/OPELIKA-AUBURN NEWS

LEFT: Auburn's Emory Blake breaks the tackle of Louisiana-Monroe's Robert Nelson.
CLIFF WILLIAMS/OPELIKA-AUBURN NEWS

BELOW: Auburn's backup quarterback Barret Trotter looks to pass. CLIFF WILLIAMS/OPELIKA-AUBURN NEWS

Kentucky vs. ⁸Auburn

October 9, 2010 • Lexington, Kentucky • W 37-34

Auburn avoids another Kentucky upset with game-winning field goal

David Morrison | Staff Writer

LEXINGTON, Ky. — The visiting team started with the ball deep in its own territory, drove methodically down the field and chewed up more than 7 minutes of clock before posting a late score to rip victory in a most excruciating fashion from the home team.

Before Saturday night, Auburn's nearest memory of a situation like that came from Alabama's 15-play, 79-yard drive that took 7:03 and ended with the touchdown that beat the Tigers in last year's Iron Bowl.

Now, Auburn's got one of its own.

The Tigers started at their own 7-yard line and went 86 yards on 19 plays, ending in a Wes Byrum 24-yard field goal as the clock struck zero to give Auburn a 37-34 win against Kentucky at Commonwealth Stadium.

Byrum's kick gave Auburn its first 6-0 start since 2004, and its senior kicker the all-time mark in career field goals with 51, passing John Vaughn.

"I had the defensive guys coming up to me, and I was telling them I was going to knock it through for them," Byrum said. "They'd been fighting all game, those guys on the O-line and D-line. The offensive line drove the ball all the way down the field and got me a short field goal for a win in the middle.

"So it really all goes to them."

Auburn (6-0, 3-0 SEC) nearly started its 19-play drive – tied for the second longest in school history – with disaster.

After Kentucky (3-3, 0-3) tied the game on a Craig McIntosh 35-yard kick with 7:31 to go, Demond Washington took the kickoff and tried to pitch to Terrell Zachery on a reverse.

The ball squirted loose, and Auburn was able to fall on it at the 7.

Two plays later, the Tigers faced a third-and-6 at their 11, but Cameron Newton found Darvin Adams — who caught five balls for 101 yards — on an out route, and the junior receiver ripped the ball from Kentucky corner Anthony Mosley's hands for 9 yards and a first down.

Auburn almost coughed it up again when Zachery fumbled on a reverse that was nearly recovered by the Wildcats but touched the sideline first — the second time the Tigers were bailed out on a fumble.

The Tigers converted two more third downs against the Wildcats, each one on a power rush by Newton, as he carried 10 times for 48 yards on the Tigers' clinching drive.

Newton had a career night for Auburn, accounting for 408 total yards — fifth on the Tigers' all-time single-game list — and four rushing touchdowns. The junior rushed 28 times for 198 yards and completed 13-of-21 passes for 210 yards and an interception.

"This guy is a worker," Auburn head coach Gene Chizik said. "He is a competitor. When the game is on the line, he wants the ball in his hands, and that's what the quarterback position should do." Auburn's epic series spoiled a spirited comeback by the home squad.

The Tigers led 31-14 after Newton capped off a magnificent first half with a 35-yard scramble, a 2-yard bull rush and a 3-yard touchdown run with 1:06 to go.

But Kentucky quarterback Mike Hartline led his team 55 yards in 59 seconds, completing 5-of-6 passes and setting up McIntosh for a 29-yarder that brought the halftime score to 31-17. Hartline completed 23-of-28 passes for 220 yards and a touchdown on the night.

As Newton and the Tigers offense struggled in the second half, Kentucky started heating up. Randall Cobb caught a 16-yard slant route for a score from Hartline, then rushed 1 yard for another score to tie the game at 31 with 4:03 in the third quarter.

Cobb ran 11 times for 47 yards and two scores, caught seven passes for 68 yards and another, and

OPPOSITE: Auburn covers a field goal by Kentucky's Spencer Holloway (83) during the Auburn-Kentucky game in Lexington, Ky. Auburn won 37-34 on kicker Wes Byrum's 24-yard field goal, to go to 6-0 on the season. VASHA HUNT/OPELIKA-AUBURN NEWS

BELOW: Auburn's Wes Byrum kicks the game-winner with two seconds left in regulation. VASHA HUNT/OPELIKA-AUBURN NEWS

threw a 6-yard touchdown to Jordan Aumiller. Byrum and McIntosh then traded field goals to set up the dramatic finish.

And all this coming on a night in which Alabama lost its first regular season game since the 2007 Iron Bowl.

"We methodically got first downs. We methodically milked the clock. We methodically did the things you have to do to win games," Chizik said. "This is kind of another one in the string of finding different ways to win." ■

RIGHT ABOVE: Aubie gives Auburn quarterback Cam Newton a big TigerWalk hug before the game. VASHA HUNT/OPELIKA-AUBURN NEWS

RIGHT BELOW: Auburn running back Michael Dyer looks for running room. VASHA HUNT/OPELIKA-AUBURN NEWS

OPPOSITE: Auburn wide receiver Kodi Burns (18) eludes a tackle after making a reception. VASHA HUNT/OPELIKA-AUBURN NEWS

BELOW: Auburn running back Onterio McCalebb breaks for open field. VASHA HUNT/OPELIKA-AUBURN NEWS

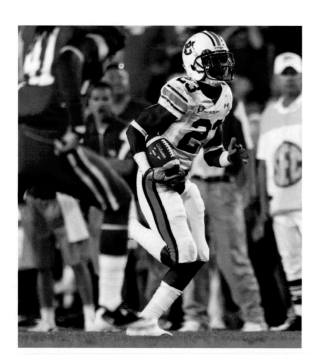

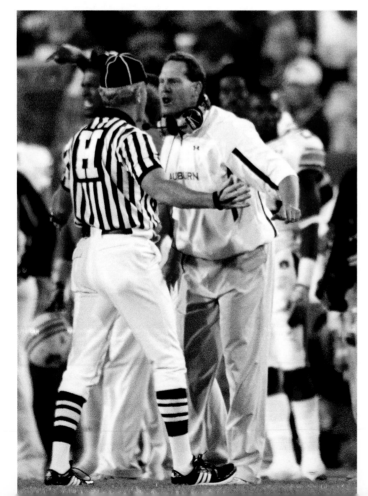

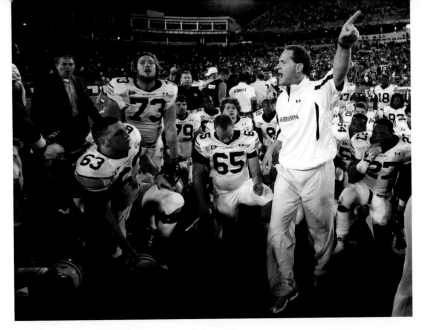

LEFT: Coach Gene Chizik tells his team to give the fans some love after the 37-34 win. VASHA HUNT/OPELIKA-AUBURN NEWS

OPPOSITE LEFT ABOVE: Auburn running back Mario Fannin (27) breaks through for red-zone yardage. VASHA HUNT/OPELIKA-AUBURN NEWS

OPPOSITE LEFT BELOW: Auburn head coach Gene Chizik argues a penalty. VASHA HUNT/OPELIKA-AUBURN NEWS

OPPOSITE RIGHT: Auburn quarterback Cam Newton (2) makes his way upfield behind the blocking of offensive lineman Mike Berry (66). VASHA HUNT/OPELIKA-AUBURN NEWS

BELOW: Cam Newton (2) and Travante Stallworth (85) celebrate with the Auburn fans at the end of the game. VASHA HUNT/OPELIKA-AUBURN NEWS

⁷Auburn vs. ¹²Arkansas

October 16, 2010 • Auburn, Alabama • W 65-43

Shootout win over Arkansas moves Auburn to 7-0

David Morrison | Staff Writer

For parts of Saturday's 65-43 win against Arkansas, Auburn's defense looked like it might struggle to slow down a pee wee football team.

A sellout Jordan-Hare Stadium crowd of 87,451 watched as Tyler Wilson, sophomore backup of the much-heralded Ryan Mallett, picked apart the No. 7 Tigers' defense after Mallett left just before halftime with a concussion after going 10-of-15 for 96 yards and a score.

Wilson, who was 1-for-3 for 6 yards and a pick this season entering the game, completed 15 of his first 17 passes for 270 yards and four touchdowns, the last coming on a 23-yard strike to Greg Childs that put No. 12 Arkansas up 43-37 early in the fourth quarter.

It turned out to be the wakeup call Auburn's defense needed, as the Tigers forced three turnovers in the final 10 minutes that played an instrumental role in extending their perfect start to 7-0.

"I was proud of their will. That's the thing our guys have is a competitive will," defensive coordinator Ted Roof said. "It's not always pretty — definitely not always pretty.

"Ugly at times."

After Cameron Newton hit Emory Blake for a 15-yard score to put the Tigers (7-0, 4-0 SEC) back on top on their next drive, Arkansas (4-2, 1-2) looked poised to strike again when Broderick Green ran for what appeared to be a first down at the Razorbacks' 47.

But the ball squirted loose — thanks to Craig Stevens, who led Auburn with 12 tackles — and Zac Etheridge scooped it up and ran 47 yards for a score to put Auburn up 50-43.

"As a defense, you look for the opportunity that we would be the reason (Auburn) would win the game," said defensive tackle Mike Blanc, who was also in on the hit. "Our main thing was the intensity of the fourth quarter.

"We knew going in that series we needed a fumble or interception."

The next time Arkansas got the ball, Wilson totally missed Josh Bynes dropping back into zone coverage, much like Stephen Garcia's freshman backup Connor Shaw did late in the Tigers' win over South Carolina.

And similar to the matchup against the Gamecocks, Bynes made the play, intercepting the ball and returning it 33 yards to the Arkansas 7.

Two plays later, Newton, who finished with a routine 188 yards and three scores on 25 carries to go along with 10-of-14 passing for 140 yards and another score, punched it in from 3 yards to put Auburn up 58-43.

The next drive, Bynes did it again, laying out for his third interception of the season and setting the table for a 38-yard Mike Dyer run for the final score in a wild game, one that set new Auburn records for points scored in an SEC game (65) and combined points (108).

"We were kidding him because last year he couldn't catch a ball," Roof said. "Couldn't catch one in practice, couldn't catch one in the games. He's catching those balls now instead of batting them to the ground.

"Thank goodness."

The stellar final 10 minutes for the Auburn defense almost overshadowed the dreadful first 50 for its head coach.

Almost.

"We struggled for a while there against a very, very good, potent offense," Gene Chizik said. "But the thing

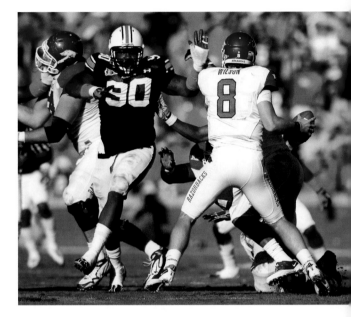

that stands out to me the most is that at the end of the game we were able to get three turnovers to change the game. What that says in my opinion is that our football team is just resilient. Our defense is resilient."

Arkansas put up 566 yards, including 428 in the air and 332 from a replacement quarterback that raised his season passer efficiency from minus-16.53 to 166.5.

Razorbacks receiver Greg Childs caught nine passes

ABOVE: Auburn defensive lineman Nick Fairley rushes Arkansas quarterback Tyler Wilson. CLIFF WILLIAMS/OPELIKA-AUBURN NEWS

OPPOSITE: Cam Newton ducks around Arkansas defenders as he looks upfield. Auburn won a wild back and forth game with a huge fourth-quarter surge, defeating Arkansas 65-43. CLIFF WILLIAMS/OPELIKA-AUBURN NEWS

for 164 yards and two scores, putting up numbers akin to the ones Gamecocks receiver Alshon Jeffery did against Auburn.

But the defense came up when it had to, and in a big way.

Chizik can add Saturday's game to his catalog of different ways Auburn has found to win games this season.

"For all of the things that we didn't do well as a team, we beat an extremely good football team tonight," Chizik said. "That's the bottom line." ∎

ABOVE: The AU flag is run across the end zone following a touchdown against Arkansas. CLIFF WILLIAMS/OPELIKA-AUBURN NEWS

RIGHT ABOVE: Cam Newton and Mario Fannin (27) celebrate a Newton touchdown. CLIFF WILLIAMS/OPELIKA-AUBURN NEWS

RIGHT: Auburn running back Onterio McCalebb (23) gets a boost from Auburn offensive lineman Ryan Pugh (50) after scoring a touchdown. VASHA HUNT/OPELIKA-AUBURN NEWS

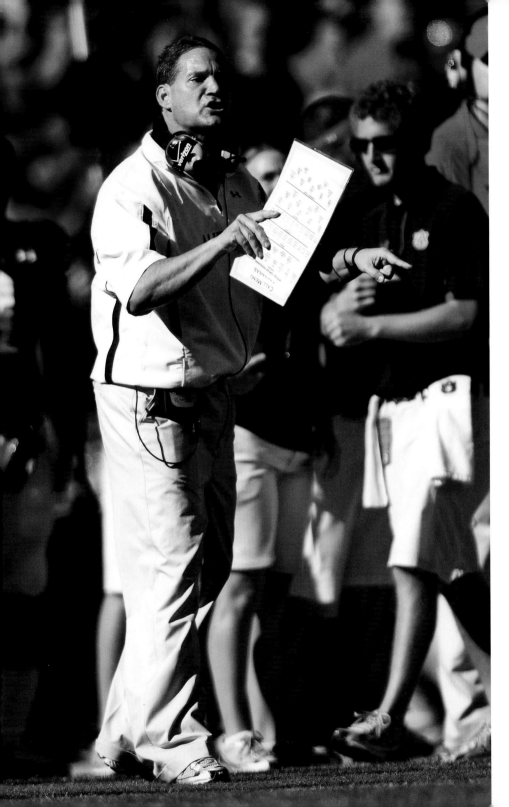

ABOVE: Nick Fairley (90) tracks Arkansas quarterback Ryan Mallett (15) on the play that appears to have knocked Mallett out of the game. VASHA HUNT/OPELIKA-AUBURN NEWS

LEFT: Auburn head coach Gene Chizik yells to the refs. VASHA HUNT/OPELIKA-AUBURN NEWS

BELOW: Cam Newton swings outside for big yardage. VASHA HUNT/OPELIKA-AUBURN NEWS

Special teams key for Tigers in win over Razorbacks

Joe McAdory | Staff Writer

J ay Boulware couldn't help but smile.
His special teams unit blocked a punt, connected on all three field goal attempts and returned a kickoff 99 yards to set up a touchdown Saturday. And his kamikaze kickoff coverage unit he proudly dubs the "Special Forces" pinned Arkansas inside its 20 six times.

"Those guys are playing their (butts) off," he beamed after the seventh-ranked Tigers' 65-43 victory Saturday at Jordan-Hare Stadium over Arkansas.

With Arkansas shredding the Auburn defense to the tune for 566 yards — a season-worst for the Tigers — it was important to pin the Razorbacks deep as often as possible.

That's where the Tigers' kickoff coverage unit comes in, specifically freshmen Demetruce McNeal and Craig Sanders and sophomores Emory Blake and Jonathan Evans, the first four inducted into Boulware's "Special Forces."

It has earned the head coach's notice.

"That team right there is filled with a bunch of freshmen, and they understand that their role this year on this football team, because we were very poor at it last year, is to gain us field position," Gene Chizik said. "You have a bunch of guys who bought into that role, but if you look real closely right now, you are going to see guys that want to be on it. They understand the importance of field position, especially when you are playing very potent offenses, and I thought they were outstanding today.

"Our special teams ... that may be one of the best special teams all around."

Aside from keeping Arkansas returners at bay, Boulware's unit provided fireworks.

Auburn had not blocked a punt since Jerraud Powers' memorable third-quarter block against Florida in 2006 in a 27-17 victory. That changed Saturday

when freshman wide receiver Antonio Goodwin burst around the edge and got a piece of Dylan Breeding's kick at the Razorback 32 in the second period. The ball ricocheted out of bounds, giving the Tigers a first down at the Arkansas 25. Three plays later, Onterio McCalebb scooted 13 yards for a touchdown, giving Auburn a 24-14 lead.

"Every week we are trying to find the weakest link in an opponent's punt coverage," Boulware said.

After Arkansas trimmed the Auburn lead to 30-28 midway into the third quarter, Boulware's unit threw another punch at the Razorbacks, this one by his kickoff return team. On a return designed to run to the right, McCalebb found a hole to the left and raced 99

yards from out of the end zone to the Arkansas 1. Two plays later, quarterback Cameron Newton scored on a keeper for a 37-28 lead.

"I cut it back to the left and it was off to the races," said McCalebb, who noted he was winded by the time he neared the goal line. "I tried to pick my legs up, but I couldn't pick them up anymore. I ran out of gas." ∎

ABOVE: Auburn defensive end Craig Sanders (13) screams after a special teams stop. VASHA HUNT/OPELIKA-AUBURN NEWS

LEFT: Cam Newton makes a towering leap for a touchdown in the third quarter. VASHA HUNT/OPELIKA-AUBURN NEWS

BELOW: Auburn wide receiver Darvin Adams (89) is hit by Arkansas cornerback Ramon Broadway (26) in the end zone, drawing a pass interference call that led to an Auburn touchdown.
VASHA HUNT/OPELIKA-AUBURN NEWS

LEFT: Auburn head coach Gene Chizik hugs his running back Michael Dyer (5) after Dyer's touchdown. VASHA HUNT/OPELIKA-AUBURN NEWS

ABOVE: Cam Newton celebrates with the fans. VASHA HUNT/OPELIKA-AUBURN NEWS

LEFT: Auburn players and fans celebrate after a wild back and forth game with a huge fourth-quarter surge. VASHA HUNT/OPELIKA-AUBURN NEWS

OPPOSITE LEFT ABOVE: Auburn defensive back Demond Washington breaks a long return. VASHA HUNT/OPELIKA-AUBURN NEWS

OPPOSITE LEFT BELOW: Auburn linebacker Josh Bynes (17) returns an interception, his first of two in the game. VASHA HUNT/OPELIKA-AUBURN NEWS

OPPOSITE RIGHT: Auburn running back Michael Dyer jogs into the end zone after ripping Arkansas's defense for a long run. VASHA HUNT/OPELIKA-AUBURN NEWS

⁵Auburn vs. ⁶LSU

October 23, 2010 • Auburn, Alabama • W 24-17

Auburn runs over, around and through LSU

David Morrison | Staff Writer

Somebody must have forgotten to tell Auburn it was going up against the third-best rush defense in the country in LSU.

The Tigers must not have been aware the Bayou Bengals hadn't allowed a 100-yard rusher all season going into Jordan-Hare Stadium on Saturday and had given up more than 100 yards to only two of the seven teams they'd faced.

Because by halftime, fourth-ranked Auburn had al-ready racked up 145 yards on the ground. By the time Onterio McCalebb took a jet sweep around the left end for a 70-yard touchdown to put Auburn up in the fourth, the Tigers had eclipsed 400 rushing yards.

And by the time Cam Newton barreled 10 yards for the game-clinching first down, taking a moment to lie on the turf and let the cheers of 87,451 wash over him, Auburn had put 440 up against the best rush defense in the SEC in a 24-17 win.

No. 6 LSU (7-1, 4-1 SEC) gave up 83.6 rush yards per game entering Saturday. That number is now 44.5 yards per game higher (128.1) thanks to Auburn (8-0, 5-0).

"I feel like that's our stat," senior guard Mike Berry said. "We don't really get any actual stats. To be able to have that many rushing yards is something that, as an offensive lineman, you take pride in." Auburn's 440 rushing yards were its most ever against an SEC opponent and its first trip above 400 since going for 405 against Mississippi State in 2003.

The catalyst, of course, was Newton.

The Heisman contender rushed 28 times for a career-high 217 yards. He is the new holder of the single-season SEC record for rushing yards by a quarterback with 1,077, breaking the 47-year old record of 1,006 set by Auburn's Jimmy Sidle.

And he's still got at least five games to go. And he still had enough energy to hurdle the 3-foot fence on the east side of the stadium to get to the fans after the game.

"I don't know," Newton said with a smile. "I think that adrenaline was still pumping."

Newton's signature run of the game — and perhaps of his Heisman campaign — came in the third quarter, when he took an inside draw, found open field, broke three or four tackles and outran everyone except LSU star corner Patrick Peterson, who he then dragged 6 yards into the end zone to put Auburn up 17-10.

That was the touchdown that broke Pat Sullivan's AU record for touchdowns accounted for in a season, 26, set in 1970.

"Plain and simple," LSU linebacker Kelvin Sheppard said. "He's the best quarterback in the country."

Mike Dyer also got into the act for Auburn, carrying 15 times for 100 yards, his first 100-yard performance since South Carolina on Sept. 25.

LEFT: Auburn quarterback Cam Newton (2) works for the game-clinching yards during the Auburn-LSU SEC game in Auburn. Fourth-ranked Auburn won the match-up of unbeatens, defeating sixth-ranked SEC rival LSU 24-17.
VASHA HUNT/OPELIKA-AUBURN NEWS

OPPOSITE: Auburn's Mario Fanin runs against LSU's Stefoin Francois.
CLIFF WILLIAMS/OPELIKA-AUBURN NEWS

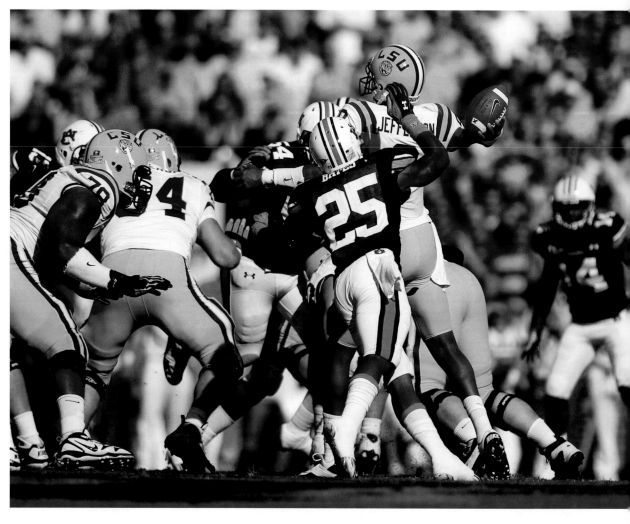

"I was going behind my tackles and they were able to open up a lot of holes for me tonight," Dyer said. "When they do that, it makes fit for easy reads. When you can read it, you just go with it. Any one of our running backs could have done what I did today."

Even with the explosive offense, even though the home Tigers outgained the visiting ones more than 2-to-1, Auburn still found itself struggling to put away LSU in the second half, thanks to some pretty ghastly field position set up by Derek Helton's clutch punting

and a timely fumble by Mario Fannin.

After Newton's highlight-reel score put Auburn back in the lead, LSU was able to play the field-position game and took over at midfield at the beginning of the fourth.

Three plays later, Spencer Ware took a lateral and lofted a 39-yard touchdown to Rueben Randle, who hauled it in over a closing Josh Bynes, to knot the score back up at 17.

That just made it all the more dramatic when Mc-

Calebb busted off left tackle 7 minutes later.

"I don't know (who) that guy was, man, for a second," Newton said. "He's running with authority now, he's not running for out of bounds. And we're going to need that from him. Everybody knows what Onterio is capable of, and tonight he showed it."

It was still up to the Auburn defense to close the game, and it did so without much of a fuss from LSU, stopping Jarrett Lee short on a fourth-down scramble.

A week after hemorrhaging 566 yards to Arkansas,

Auburn's defense held LSU to 234 — its lowest yield of the season — recording nine tackles for loss and three sacks.

Nick Fairley happily contributed 2.5 of those sacks and 3.5 of those TFLs, extending his league-leading total to 17 for the season.

"We've had some stretches where we haven't played very well and we've had some stretches where we've done some wonderful things," defensive coordinator Ted Roof said. "Just because we played well today doesn't mean we've arrived." ■

ABOVE: Auburn cheerleaders wave the flags after the touchdown by Cam Newton. VASHA HUNT/OPELIKA-AUBURN NEWS

OPPOSITE LEFT ABOVE: A Navy F-18 flies over Jordan-Hare. VASHA HUNT/OPELIKA-AUBURN NEWS

OPPOSITE LEFT BELOW: Auburn safety Zac Etheridge plays to the crowd. VASHA HUNT/OPELIKA-AUBURN NEWS

OPPOSITE RIGHT: Auburn's Daren Bates puts pressure on LSU quarterback Jordan Jefferson. CLIFF WILLIAMS/OPELIKA-AUBURN NEWS

LEFT: Cam Newton eludes LSU defensive end Kendrick Adams for positive yardage in the first half. VASHA HUNT/OPELIKA-AUBURN NEWS

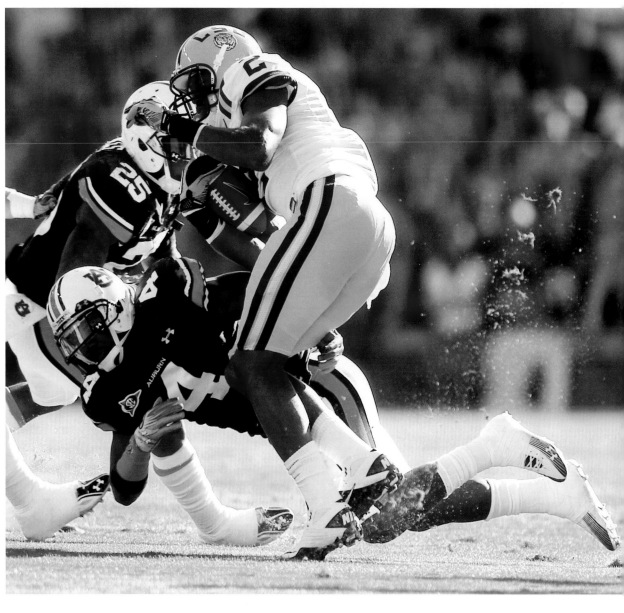

ABOVE: Zac Etheridge (4) cuts down LSU wide receiver Rueben Rueben Randle. CLIFF WILLIAMS/OPELIKA-AUBURN NEWS

LEFT ABOVE: Auburn wide receiver Terrell Zachery (81) gets into the secondary. VASHA HUNT/OPELIKA-AUBURN NEWS

LEFT: Auburn running back Michael Dyer hits a hole. VASHA HUNT/OPELIKA-AUBURN NEWS

LEFT ABOVE: Michael Dyer (5) finds open field for a big gain. VASHA HUNT/OPELIKA-AUBURN NEWS

OPPOSITE LEFT ABOVE: Auburn fans cheer quarterback Cam Newton (2) after his second TD run. VASHA HUNT/OPELIKA-AUBURN NEWS

OPPOSITE RIGHT ABOVE: LSU Head Coach Les Miles yells to his players. VASHA HUNT/OPELIKA-AUBURN NEWS

OPPOSITE BELOW: Auburn running back Onterio McCalebb (23) takes off on a 70-yard TD run. VASHA HUNT/OPELIKA-AUBURN NEWS

LEFT BELOW: Auburn wide receiver Darvin Adams (89) works for reception yards as LSU safety Craig Loston (6) hits him. VASHA HUNT/OPELIKA-AUBURN NEWS

LEFT: Auburn fans cheer quarterback Cam Newton after his second touchdown run. VASHA HUNT/OPELIKA-AUBURN NEWS

BELOW: Auburn running back Onterio McCalebb (23) avoids the grasp of LSU safety Brandon Taylor (15) and takes off on a 70-yard touchdown run. VASHA HUNT/OPELIKA-AUBURN NEWS

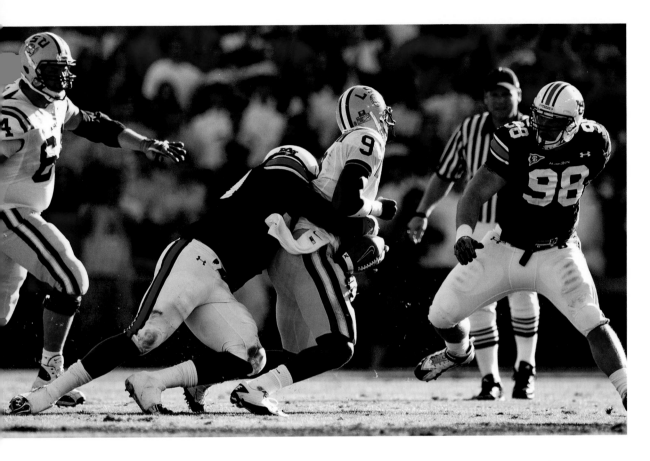

Fairley helps Auburn defense stop LSU

Joe McAdory | Staff Writer

Even Cam Newton doesn't want any part of Nick Fairley.

"He's a big human being," the Auburn quarterback and Heisman Trophy candidate said Saturday after the fourth-ranked Tigers' 24-17 win. "I wouldn't want to face that guy." LSU, however, did.

Fairley, a junior defensive tackle, registered 2.5 sacks and 3.5 tackles for loss (Auburn had nine total) as the Tiger defense enjoyed its most productive game of the season – holding sixth-ranked LSU to just 243 yards. Auburn held Mississippi State to 246 yards on Sept. 11.

"It all starts up front," said Auburn defensive coordinator Ted Roof. "He (Fairley) is the centerpiece to that. We got pressure today with the front four and that makes things easier." LSU quarterbacks Jarrett Lee and Jordan Jefferson combined for 128 passing yards and faced constant pressure. Fairley leveled Lee — hard — twice after Lee released the ball, once sending Lee to the sideline holding his wrist.

"We went into halftime and said that we have to get the quarterback if we are going to win this game," Fairley said.

Auburn head coach Gene Chizik considered Fairley a "dominant force."

"Nick, I thought, took the game over inside," he said.

Fairley's presence was never more evident than on LSU's next-to-last possession. With the score knotted at 17, Fairley stuffed LSU running back Stevan Ridley for a 3-yard loss back to the Bayou Bengal 37. Two plays later on third-and-6, Fairley leveled Jefferson for a 9-yard loss.

Moments later, Auburn running back Onterio McCalebb zipped 70 yards for the game-winning touchdown and LSU never threatened again.

"Going back out there after Onterio scored, we knew that if we made the stop we were going to win," Fairley said. "We just ran our base defense and were in the right place at the right time to make plays."

With defensive back regulars T'Sharvan Bell and Aairon Savage out Saturday with injuries, Auburn turned to the bench for help in the secondary.

True freshman cornerback Chris Davis registered three tackles and defended a pass, while walk-on safety Ikeem Means played but did not have a tackle.

"We always want to step up for a challenge," said Davis. "That's how I took it. Coach said that I had to step up. Sometimes you take it as motivation. Tonight, I answered the challenge."

Senior linebacker Josh Bynes, who led all tacklers with 11, was relieved the defense "put together four quarters."

"Everyone thought it was going to be a high-scoring game," he said. "We played like every down was our last and we kept thinking about three-and-outs. We figured out their gameplan and got to it. It's a great feeling ... to hold them to that many yards. It was our best game defensively this year."

Auburn came into Saturday's contest on the heels of allowing potent Arkansas 566 yards in a 65-43 shootout. The Tigers were ranked eighth in the SEC in total defense (383 ypg) and dead last in pass defense (272 ypg) in conference games.

"We knew, as a secondary, that we needed to step up and play better than we did last week against Arkansas," said senior safety Zac Etheridge. "We just went out there and played." ∎

ABOVE: Auburn defensive lineman Nick Fairley hits LSU quarterback Jordan Jefferson (9). VASHA HUNT/OPELIKA-AUBURN NEWS

ABOVE: Onterio McCalebb outruns LSU cornerback Patrick Peterson for a 70-yard touchdown. VASHA HUNT/OPELIKA-AUBURN NEWS

RIGHT: Cam Newton (2) goes airborn for yards.
VASHA HUNT/OPELIKA-AUBURN NEWS

FAR RIGHT: Cam Newton celebrates with adoring Auburn fans in the northwest corner after the game. VASHA HUNT/OPELIKA-AUBURN NEWS

BELOW: LSU running back Stevan Ridley sits dazed after a hard hit from Auburn linebacker Josh Bynes. VASHA HUNT/OPELIKA-AUBURN NEWS

Mississippi vs. ³Auburn

October 30, 2010 • Oxford, Mississippi • W 51-31

New-look offense leads Tigers to statement win

David Morrison | Staff Writer

OXFORD, Miss. — Yes, he can throw, too. And he can run routes, post up a cornerback, make a catch and get two feet in bounds in the corner of the end zone.

No. 1 Auburn seemed dead set on proving its Heisman Trophy contender Cam Newton was more than just a running quarterback in its 51-31 romp against Ole Miss in front of 61,474 fans at Vaught-Hemingway Stadium on Saturday night, the fifth-largest crowd in Ole Miss program history.

Newton completed 18-of-24 passes for 209 yards and two scores on the night and ran only 11 times for 45 yards.

He tied his season high in pass attempts by halftime at 21 and provided a strong counterpoint to the past three SEC games, in which he averaged 201 rush yards and 145.3 yards passing.

"We have an excellent passing attack that is capable of striking at any time," Newton said. "A lot of people hadn't really seen that, because we hadn't pulled that rabbit out of our hats yet."

The Tigers (9-0, 5-0 SEC) showed their dedication to the pass from their first snap, as Newton completed 3-of-3 attempts for 37 yards on the first three plays.

Then, on the sixth play of the drive, he lined out wide against Ole Miss cornerback Jeremy McGee — who was giving up 8 inches and 70 pounds on him — and Kodi Burns lofted a pass in his direction.

Newton got position on McGee, made the grab and dragged both feet in the corner for a 20-yard score that evened the game, after Jeff Scott started it off with some fireworks on an 83-yard touchdown run for the Rebels (3-5, 1-4).

"It's hard to defend a 6-6 receiver ... or quarterback," Auburn coach Gene Chizik said with a wry grin. "Whatever you want to call it."

Auburn also went to Newton's arm to cap off its most emphatic drive of the evening, one that began on a Demond Washington pick at its own 2-yard line.

Ole Miss had taken over at the Auburn 18 after a fumble — trailing 17-14 — and quarterback Jeremiah Masoli tried twice to beat Washington on a fade route, much the same route the Rebels used to burn him on a Markeith Summers 29-yard scoring grab in the first.

But Washington was ready.

"I knew after the touchdown pass, they were going to feel like it would be there all night," Washington said. "I was waiting on it. I was hoping they were going to throw it." Auburn took over at the 2 and drove 98 yards in 12 plays, tied for the fourth-longest drive in program history, with the last 24 coming on a Newton pass to Darvin Adams.

Adams had been mostly a blocker in the two games previous, catching five passes for 67 yards. He caught six for 75 on Saturday.

"Each week, you see what they're giving you," offensive coordinator Gus Malzahn said. "They weren't rushing, they were squeezing everything down. They were giving us the pass."

The Tigers' defense also made its presence known shortly before the half, stopping Masoli on a fourth-and-1 and giving the offense time to set up a Wes Byrum 35-yard field goal that brought them into the break up 34-17.

Auburn's defense allowed just 32 yards and one first down in the third quarter, as the offense put the game away with 10 points of its own.

"Our message at halftime was: 'These guys aren't going to go away,'" Chizik said. "We had to come out with a fast start, both sides of the football."

Auburn reverted to its smashmouth form of late in the second half, but it was weapons other than Newton making an impact as the Rebels keyed in on him.

Namely, freshman Mike Dyer, who rushed for a career-high 180 yards on 21 carries, with a 30-yard touchdown run.

The Tigers ran 25 times for 203 yards in the second half, racking up 343 rush yards on the game – their fifth straight SEC game over 300 – and 572 total yards.

"Any time you see a smile on (Malzahn), you know you achieved something," Newton said. "And I saw a lot of smiles in him tonight." ∎

OPPOSITE: Auburn wide receiver Darvin Adams makes an over-the-shoulder catch for a touchdown as Ole Miss cornerback Jeremy McGee can't break up the play during the Auburn's game against 'Ole Miss in Oxford, Miss. VASHA HUNT/OPELIKA-AUBURN NEWS

BELOW: Auburn defensive back Demond Washington (14) breaks a 95-yard kickoff return for a touchdown. VASHA HUNT/OPELIKA-AUBURN NEWS

ABOVE: Auburn running back Onterio McCalebb (23) and defensive lineman Brandon Mosley (75) celebrate a long touchdown run as senior offensive lineman Lee Ziemba (73) looks on.
VASHA HUNT/OPELIKA-AUBURN NEWS

LEFT ABOVE: Auburn quarterback Cam Newton catches a touchdown pass over the much shorter Ole Miss cornerback Jeremy McGee. The pass was thrown by Auburn wide receiver Kodi Burns.
VASHA HUNT/OPELIKA-AUBURN NEWS

LEFT: Onterio McCalebb outruns Ole Miss cornerback Marcus Temple for a touchdown.
VASHA HUNT/OPELIKA-AUBURN NEWS

LEFT: Auburn running back Michael Dyer (5) avoids an Ole Miss defender to break a long run. VASHA HUNT/OPELIKA-AUBURN NEWS

BELOW: Demond Washington (14) sees nothing but open field in front of him as he returns a kickoff 95 yards for an Auburn touchdown. VASHA HUNT/OPELIKA-AUBURN NEWS

Tigers get job done through the air

Mike Szvetitz | Staff Writer

OXFORD, Miss. — The last few games, Auburn's wideouts have been receiving a lot of praise for their blocking.

What they haven't been getting is the football.

That changed Saturday.

In the Tigers' 51-31 win over the Rebels, four different Tiger wideouts caught 18 passes for 229 yards.

"We kind of took what the defense gave us," junior Darvin Adams said. "They tired to stuff the box with a lot of people in there. I think Coach (Gus) Malzahn did a great job picking the defense apart." Adams led Auburn with six catches for 75 yards and a touchdown, while Emory Blake and Terrell Zachery snagged five passes each. Kodi Burns rounded out the night with two catches.

It was part of Malzahn's gameplan to go to the air, with the Rebels focused on stopping Auburn quarterback Cam Newton, who came into Saturday's game averaging 134 yards rushing per game.

And it worked. At first.

"They just took (Newton's) run away," Malzahn said. "All his read stuff, they were making him give it. Which slowed him down on the rush, but we were able to do some things in the passing game." Which was just fine with Adams and Co.

"Of course, we're receivers," Adams said. "We practice catching the ball every day."

This was the third-most passing yards the Tigers have put up this season, with the first two coming against Arkansas State and ULM – not exactly SEC defenses.

"It was good that we spread the ball around," Malzahn, Auburn's offensive coordinator, said. "A lot of different guys touched it, which is good. And that makes it much tougher on defenses later on."

One man defenses have to keep tabs on is Adams, Auburn's leading receiver. The junior now has 32 catches on the season for 527 yards and three touchdowns.

He's become Newton's go-to guy on third downs, as most of Adams' catches have come on those series-deciding snaps.

"Cam's got a lot of trust in me, as well as Coach Malzahn, and plus, myself, I want the ball, too," Adams said. "Cam's giving me a chance, you know, throwing it around. I just got to make a play."

But that's not to say that Auburn didn't run the football in Saturday's win. After Newton softened up the Rebels with his arm, the legs of Auburn's running backs went to work.

True freshman Mike Dyer ran the ball 21 times for 180 yards and a score, while Onterio McCalebb was just 1 yard shy of the century mark on nine carries. ∎

ABOVE: Auburn wide receiver Terrell Zachery (81) scores on a fourth-quarter reception to push the Tigers' score to 51.
VASHA HUNT/OPELIKA-AUBURN NEWS

ABOVE: Auburn running back Michael Dyer burns yards and clock late in the fourth quarter. VASHA HUNT/OPELIKA-AUBURN NEWS

LEFT ABOVE: Auburn defensive back Demond Washington crosses the goal line at the end of his 95-yard kickoff return.
VASHA HUNT/OPELIKA-AUBURN NEWS

LEFT: Cam Newton celebrates with fans in the stands after the 51-31 win.
VASHA HUNT/OPELIKA-AUBURN NEWS

November 6, 2010 • Auburn, Alabama • W 62-24

Newton: I feel 10-0

David Morrison | Staff Writer

Cam Newton walked into the postgame interview room with a smile on his face Saturday.

The junior quarterback seemed exactly the same after No. 2 Auburn's 62-24 win over Chattanooga — just two days after an ESPN.com story linked his name with an NCAA investigation — as he has been all season.

"I feel 10-0," he said, with a grin. "I'm just ecstatic. I'm dumbfounded with what words to say to express my emotion with how great I feel right now."

With Alabama's 24-21 loss to LSU on Saturday, Auburn only needs to beat Georgia next week to clinch a spot in the SEC championship game.

Newton set an Auburn career high with 317 passing yards and four touchdowns, completing 15-of-21 attempts — all in the first half — as the Tigers ran out to a 48-14 lead at the break against Chattanooga (5-4).

It was the most points in a first half for Auburn (10-0) since scoring 49 in a 76-10 win over Chattanooga (5-4) in 1995.

Media members were cautioned before Newton's interview to keep all discussion "football-related," but he still fielded questions about the report alleging someone was shopping him around to FBS schools during his recruitment last year.

"I wish I could talk about it right now, but I can't," Newton said. "That's the way it is."

When pressed on the issue, Newton replied, "I haven't done anything wrong."

"God is blessing me right in my life and the way I play, and I'll always owe that to Him," Newton said. "When God be blessing, the devil be messing."

Tigers head coach Gene Chizik said he couldn't talk about the incident but reiterated his statement from Thursday night: "Cameron Newton is eligible at Auburn. He played today and he played great. And that's where we're going to let it lie."

He was a bit more loquacious on the subject of Newton's character.

"Let me tell you something. This is a great kid," Chizik said. "I can speak intelligently on that one. And you can go back and you can talk to elementary coaches, high school, this is a great kid and he's been a great kid at Auburn University every day he's been around me, this staff and his teammates.

"I don't know what's out there, but I can assure you this: this is a phenomenal young man. Make no mistake about that."

Any questions of how the hectic past two days would take a toll on Newton's play were laid to rest in the first 30 seconds, when he slung a screen pass out to Terrell Zachery for 32 yards then hit Darvin Adams over the top for a 30-yard touchdown to put Auburn up, 7-0.

By the end of the first quarter, he had completed 9-of-14 passes for 193 yards and three touchdowns — two to Adams and one to Emory Blake — and a 1-yard touchdown run.

By the end of the half, he added another touchdown toss to Zachery, who finished with seven catches for 148 yards. The Tigers had 484 yards of total offense, and Newton's day was done.

"Just very Cameron-like, if you will," Chizik said.

Chizik said he had met with the team to discuss Newton's situation but declined to share details of the meeting.

Newton's teammates appeared unaware of the storm surrounding the Heisman contender.

"I'm not too familiar with all that," defensive end Antoine Carter said.

Chizik said reacting to outside perception, or maintaining an "us against the world" mentality, has never been a strong suit of his team.

"That's not how we live our life. That's not who we are," Chizik said. "Here's who we are. Every day as a football team, as a team, as a family, we try to improve.

OPPOSITE: Auburn's Terrell Zachery scores a first-half touchdown against Chattanooga. CLIFF WILLIAMS/OPELIKA-AUBURN NEWS

BELOW: Auburn quarterback Cam Newton responds to questions from the media after the Auburn-Chattanooga homecoming football game in Auburn. Auburn won 62-24 to go to 10-0 on the year. VASHA HUNT/OPELIKA-AUBURN NEWS

Whatever is out there is out there and we're going to stay focused and we're going to do what we are supposed to do to be a better football team.

"That's all that matters."

Newton left the podium and headed back to the locker room, head bobbing slightly and a look of calm on his face.

"I'm not here to tell people what I can do on the field," Newton said. "It's just my heart, and what I can for people as a person.

"At the end of the day, I lay my head down just as normal as you all." ∎

RIGHT ABOVE: Fans cheer for Auburn. VASHA HUNT/OPELIKA-AUBURN NEWS

RIGHT BELOW: Cam Newton launches a pass against Chattanooga. CLIFF WILLIAMS/OPELIKA-AUBURN NEWS

OPPOSITE: Auburn's Onterioo McCalebb cuts upfield. CLIFF WILLIAMS/OPELIKA-AUBURN NEWS

BELOW: Tigerette and Auburn senior Alexandra Sabates shows her support for Cam Newton. VASHA HUNT/OPELIKA-AUBURN NEWS

ABOVE: Auburn running back Onterio McCalebb (23) breaks a tackle to move for a solid gain. VASHA HUNT/OPELIKA-AUBURN NEWS

RIGHT ABOVE: Cam Newton hurdles Chattanooga linebacker J.D. Dothard. VASHA HUNT/OPELIKA-AUBURN NEWS

RIGHT: Auburn running back Michael Dyer (5) breaks loose for an easy touchdown run. VASHA HUNT/OPELIKA-AUBURN NEWS

ABOVE: Auburn's Mario Fannin tries to bream free of a Chattanooga defender.
CLIFF WILLIAMS/OPELIKA-AUBURN NEWS

LEFT: Auburn defensive end Corey Lemonier hits Chattanooga quarterback B.J. Coleman.
VASHA HUNT/OPELIKA-AUBURN NEWS

BELOW: Cam Newton celebrates with AU fans.
VASHA HUNT/OPELIKA-AUBURN NEWS

November 13, 2010 • Auburn, Alabama • W 49-31

Newton plays, leads Auburn to SEC West title

David Morrison | Staff Writer

Darvin Adams, Daren Bates, Nick Fairley, Cam Newton and others joined the band's front row, making up a navy blue mass as the brass carried the fight song.

Kodi Burns, Byron Isom, Ryan Pugh and Lee Ziemba mounted the cheerleaders' makeshift stage on the east side of Jordan-Hare Stadium, leading Auburn fans in a chorus of "Lean on Me."

The Tigers' seniors took a victory lap around Jordan-Hare Stadium as season highlights beamed on the big screen in the south end zone.

Highlights from their run to the SEC championship game.

No. 2 Auburn sewed up the SEC West championship and a trip to Atlanta to take on South Carolina with a 49-31 win over Georgia on Saturday in front of 87,451 fans at Jordan-Hare Stadium.

It's the Tigers' first division title since 2004, a year in which they won the SEC championship and finished 13-0.

"It is a great thing especially for the guys that have been here for four or five years," linebacker Josh Bynes said. "A lot of guys have been through three or four offensive and defensive coordinators, but with having the same staff from last year, we felt that we were going to go from good to great. We felt that we had a chance to go undefeated.

"Right now we are sitting at 11-0 and sitting as the SEC West champions."

Auburn beat the Bulldogs (5-6) in much the same fashion as it has handled opponents all year — with the legs of Cam Newton.

Newton, whose eligibility status was thrown into question after new allegations that his father, Cecil Newton Sr., sought money from Mississippi State during the quarterback's recruitment last year, accounted for 299 total yards and four touchdowns Saturday.

Multiple media outlets reported Saturday morning that Newton and his family met with NCAA investiga-

OPPOSITE: Cam Newton (2), Daren Bates (25), and Onterio McCalebb (23) celebrate with the fans after the Auburn-Georgia SEC football game in Auburn. Auburn clinched the SEC West with a 49-31 victory over the Bulldogs. VASHA HUNT/OPELIKA-AUBURN NEWS

BELOW: Auburn defensive linemen Mike Blanc (93) and Nick Fairley (90) celebrate with fans. VASHA HUNT/OPELIKA-AUBURN NEWS

tors this week, and the initial round of questioning revealed Newton knew nothing of his father's request.

Auburn head coach Gene Chizik only took questions about Newton's performance Saturday in his postgame press conference, and Newton was not made available for comment.

Newton rushed a season-high 30 times for 151 yards and two scores and completed 12-of-15 passes for 148 yards, two touchdowns and an interception.

With his 18-yard touchdown toss to Philip Lutzenkirchen in the first half, Newton became the first player in SEC history to total 2,000 passing yards and 1,000 rushing yards in a season.

Newton now stands at 2,038 yards and 21 touchdowns passing to go along with 1,297 yards and 17 scores on the ground.

Lutzenkirchen's touchdown grab capped off a 14-point comeback for the Tigers, who trailed 21-7 after a 40-yard touchdown pass from Aaron Murray to A.J. Green with 1:00 to go in the first quarter.

Green lit up the Auburn secondary for 164 yards and two scores on nine catches. But he had only 50 yards after halftime.

"We did a good job of, when we weren't sacking (Murray), we were at least pressuring him in the pocket," defensive coordinator Ted Roof said. "He couldn't just sit back and pat the ball and wait for A.J. Green to come open. He did that enough in the first half."

Wes Byrum recovered an onside kick to start the second half, and Auburn took the lead on an Onterio McCalebb touchdown run, his second of three on the day.

Georgia answered back with a 7-yard run by Washaun Ealey, but the Tigers outscored the Bulldogs,

RIGHT ABOVE: Cam Newton works the crowd at TigerWalk before the game. VASHA HUNT/OPELIKA-AUBURN NEWS

RIGHT: The Auburn University Marching Band takes the field at Jordan-Hare Stadium prior to the game. CLIFF WILLIAMS/OPELIKA-AUBURN NEWS

FAR RIGHT: Auburn coach Gus Malzahn huddles with his quarterbacks prior to the game. CLIFF WILLIAMS/OPELIKA-AUBURN NEWS

ABOVE: Auburn running back Michael Dyer eludes Georgia linebacker Akeem Dent. VASHA HUNT/OPELIKA-AUBURN NEWS

21-3, down the stretch, with a 13-yard, fourth-quarter toss from Newton to Lutzenkirchen sliding the dagger in.

Auburn controlled the tempo offensively in the second half, running for 186 of its 315 yards after the break.

"After we kept pounding them, they got more and more tired," guard Mike Berry said. "We were able to wear them down."

The Tigers now get their first off-week of the season, then the Iron Bowl and then a rematch with the Gamecocks on Dec. 4, who they beat 35-27 earlier this season.

For now, though, senior safety Zac Etheridge said he's going to take a moment to cherish Jordan-Hare sending him out a champion.

"I had to go around the stadium three or four times at the end," Etheridge said. "You'll never experience anything like this ever again. I'm glad for the Auburn Family. I'm going to miss it and I've enjoyed it." ■

ABOVE: Auburn's Craig Sanders celebrates a stop against Georgia.

CLIFF WILLIAMS/OPELIKA-AUBURN NEWS

RIGHT ABOVE: Auburn tackle Nick Fairley, named the winner of the Vince Lombardi Award for college football's most outstanding linemen, focuses on Georgia's offense. CLIFF WILLIAMS/OPELIKA-AUBURN NEWS

RIGHT: Auburn linebacker Daren Bates brings down Georgia quarterback Aaron Murray. CLIFF WILLIAMS/OPELIKA-AUBURN NEWS

OPPOSITE LEFT: Auburn's Emory Blake is unable to come up with the catch. CLIFF WILLIAMS/OPELIKA-AUBURN NEWS

OPPOSITE RIGHT ABOVE: Cam Newton looks downfield for an open receiver as Byron Isom blocks. CLIFF WILLIAMS/OPELIKA-AUBURN NEWS

OPPOSITE RIGHT BELOW: Auburn's Mario Fannin is brought down by Georgia inside linebacker Akeen Dent. CLIFF WILLIAMS/OPELIKA-AUBURN NEWS

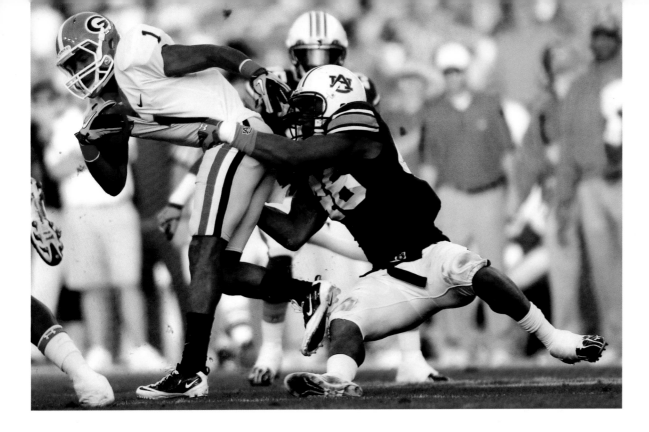

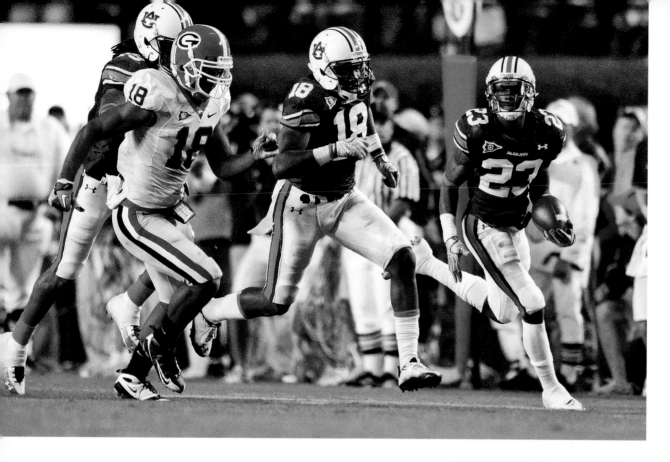

ABOVE: Auburn running back Onterio McCalebb (23) runs downfield, escorted by wide receiver Kodi Burns (18). VASHA HUNT/OPELIKA-AUBURN NEWS

RIGHT ABOVE: Cam Newton (2) congratulates Onterio McCalebb (23) on his touchdown run. VASHA HUNT/OPELIKA-AUBURN NEWS

RIGHT: Onterio McCalebb steps across the goal line as Georgia cornerback Brandon Boykin is too late to stop him. VASHA HUNT/OPELIKA-AUBURN NEWS

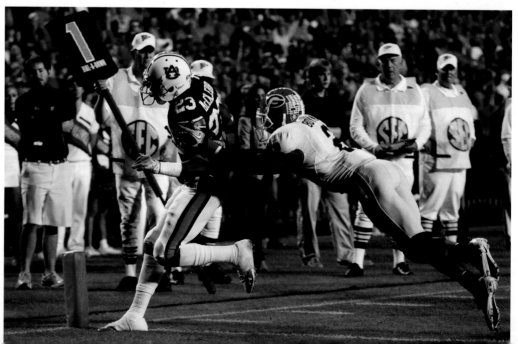

LEFT: Auburn defensive lineman Nick Fairley (90) celebrates after sacking Georgia quarterback Aaron Murray on 4th down. VASHA HUNT/OPELIKA-AUBURN NEWS

BELOW: Cam Newton (2) scores over the top for the final touchdown of the game. VASHA HUNT/OPELIKA-AUBURN NEWS

ABOVE: Auburn wide receiver Kodi Burns celebrates with fans after his final home game. VASHA HUNT/OPELIKA-AUBURN NEWS

RIGHT: Fans cheer Auburn seniors as they celebrate after their last game in Jordan-Hare Stadium. VASHA HUNT/OPELIKA-AUBURN NEWS

BELOW: Auburn offensive lineman Lee Ziemba celebrates with fans after the game. VASHA HUNT/OPELIKA-AUBURN NEWS

I flew from Lubbock 1,049 MI to see CAM Newton

⁹Alabama vs. ²Auburn

November 26, 2010 • Tuscaloosa, Alabama • W 28-27

Tigers rally back from 24-points down to beat Alabama in Iron Bowl

David Morrison | Staff Writer

TUSCALOOSA — The Auburn halftime locker room was neither jubilant nor morose Friday, with the team trailing by 17 with only 30 minutes left on the clock to try to preserve its undefeated season.

Tigers players were even-keel, expectant, cognizant of the challenge that awaited them but confident that — if this season has shown them anything — they were up for it.

Or in the words of quarterback Cam Newton: "We comin'."

"A lot of seniors stepped up, Cam stepped up and said some things," said safety Zac Etheridge, speaking for Newton as the quarterback entered Day 17 of media silence. "We didn't let the storm weather us.

"(Newton) didn't say much, just 'Keep on. We comin'.' We feed off of him, saying 'We comin'.'"

No. 2 Auburn was, in fact, coming, taking control of the game from the second snap of the second half and overcoming its fourth double-digit deficit of the season in a 28-27 win in front of 101,821 stunned fans at Bryant-Denny Stadium.

The Tigers (12-0, 8-0 SEC) kept their hopes for a national championship alive by staging the biggest comeback in program history against their biggest foe.

All in all, one of the most important wins ever at Auburn.

"Sometimes it's not just that you win. Sometimes a lot is about how you win," head coach Gene Chizik

said. "I don't think anybody that saw that game can deny it was not just a win. It was about how we won."

Auburn seemed a long shot to win, to even hang with No. 10 Alabama (9-3, 5-3) for most of the first half, as the Crimson Tide racked up 379 yards.

Quarterback Greg McElroy passed for a career-high 335 yards in the first 30 minutes. Julio Jones hauled in seven passes for 174 yards.

Auburn showed all the signs of a team getting blown out of its rival's building as it fell behind 24-7 at the break.

But with two huge turnovers, the Tigers had something to hang their hats on.

The first came via Antoine Carter, who socked the ball from Mark Ingram's arms at the tail end of a 41-yard gain and out the back of the end zone for a touchback. Alabama could have gone up 28-0 with a touchdown there.

"(Ingram) started to pull off," Carter said. "I just kept running and, you know, when you finish plays great things happen."

The second came from Nick Fairley, who sacked McElroy on second-and-goal at the 8, forced a fumble and recovered it. Alabama would have been ahead 31-7 with a touchdown there.

"It was just wide open: a three-step drop and he was just right there," Fairley said. "When he fell, the offensive line was trying to help him up and the play was still going on. I just saw the ball was rolling around, so I jumped on it.

"We got the dog in us. We're going to always fight."

Auburn started flipping the script with a 70-yard touchdown strike from Newton to Terrell Zachery on the second play out of the break, one in which safety Mark Barron looked lost.

The Tigers followed that up with a 75-yard drive ending in a Newton plunge to cut the lead to 24-21 with 4:25 to go in the third.

After a Jeremy Shelley field goal extended the Crimson Tide lead to 6, Auburn drove 67 yards — including a fourth-and-3 conversion — ending in a 7-yard pass from Newton to Philip Lutzenkirchen to put it up with 11:55 left in the game.

"We came here to win the game," Chizik said. "We did not come here to tie. We did not come here with our hat in our hands. We came here to win the game. I have much faith in our guys on fourth-and-3 as anybody in the planet."

ABOVE: Alabama quarterback Greg McElroy drops back to pass during the Auburn-Alabama Ironbowl game in Tuscaloosa. Auburn needed a major comeback to win 28-27 and go 12-0 on the year.
VASHA HUNT/OPELIKA-AUBURN NEWS

OPPOSITE: Aubie celebrates with the team after the game.
VASHA HUNT/OPELIKA-AUBURN NEWS

Newton finished 13-of-20 for 216 yards and three touchdowns and ran 22 times for 39 yards and another score in the win.

Alabama drove to the edge of field-goal range in its next trip down the field, but a 2-yard loss on an Ingram run and a 4-yard loss on a T'Sharvan Bell sack of McElroy led to a punt.

McElroy left with what Alabama coach Nick Saban called a concussion after the hit, and Alabama couldn't muster anything with backup A.J. McCarron in its last-ditch effort.

McElroy went 8-of-14 for 42 yards in the second half to finish 27-of-37 passing for 377 yards. Jones caught three balls for 24 yards after the break to finish with 10 catches for 199 yards.

Auburn's defense held the Crimson Tide to just 67 yards in the second half.

"We're definitely a second-half defense. I don't think there's any question about that," defensive coordinator Ted Roof said. "Their ability to handle the adjustments and take them onto the field, that's what they did."

On the same field in which it suffered a 36-0 loss two years ago, to the same team against which it swallowed the bitter pill of a 26-21 defeat last year, Auburn celebrated Friday.

For the 13th straight week, the Tigers remain undefeated.

"We get the job done in the second half," Etheridge said. "We know every game we come out here to finish. And that's what we do." ∎

TOP: Auburn quarterback Cameron Newton points to the fans as the game begins. VASHA HUNT/OPELIKA-AUBURN NEWS

BOTTOM LEFT: Alabama running back Mark Ingram (22) scores a touchdown and revs up the Alabama fans. VASHA HUNT/OPELIKA-AUBURN NEWS

BOTTOM RIGHT: Mark Ingram celebrates his touchdown. VASHA HUNT/OPELIKA-AUBURN NEWS

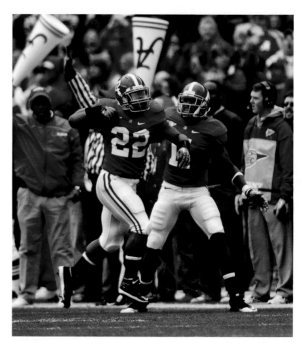

ABOVE: Alabama quarterback Greg McElroy (12) plays to the crowd as the Crimson Tide goes up by 21 points. VASHA HUNT/OPELIKA-AUBURN NEWS

TOP LEFT: Alabama wide receiver Julio Jones (8) scores a touchdown as Alabama fans celebrate. VASHA HUNT/OPELIKA-AUBURN NEWS

BOTTOM LEFT: Alabama's Greg McElroy and wide receiver Earl Alexander hug Alabama wide receiver Julio Jones after his touchdown reception. VASHA HUNT/OPELIKA-AUBURN NEWS

BELOW: Alabama wide receiver Darius Hanks burns Auburn defensive back Neiko Thorpe for a touchdown reception. VASHA HUNT/OPELIKA-AUBURN NEWS

ABOVE: Frenzied Alabama fans celebrate Alabama's surge in the first half of one of the greatest Iron Bowl games ever played.   VASHA HUNT/OPELIKA-AUBURN NEWS

ABOVE: Auburn defensive lineman Nick Fairley (90) wraps up Alabama running back Trent Richardson (3). VASHA HUNT/OPELIKA-AUBURN NEWS

LEFT: Auburn Head Coach Gene Chizik tries to figure out what is going on as his team falls behind in the first half. VASHA HUNT/OPELIKA-AUBURN NEWS

BELOW: Auburn wide receiver Emory Blake (80) beats Alabama defensive back Mark Barron (4) for Auburn's lone touchdown in the first half. VASHA HUNT/OPELIKA-AUBURN NEWS

RIGHT: Auburn Head Coach Gene Chizik, named National Coach of the Year after the season, is all business in the second half. VASHA HUNT/OPELIKA-AUBURN NEWS

OPPOSITE: Cam Newton signals in the red zone during the second half. VASHA HUNT/OPELIKA-AUBURN NEWS

Tigers find a way ... all the way to 12-0

Mike Szvetitz | Sports Editor

TUSCALOOSA — Gene Chizik was non-committal.

The biggest win he's ever been a part of?

"It's certainly up there," Auburn's head coach said. "It's certainly up there."

Granted, Chizik, who's 20-5 as Auburn's head coach, has been a part of some very big wins, including a national championship victory as the defensive coordinator at Texas.

But to be down 24 points at your rival's stadium with everything this game had riding on it?

How could it not be the biggest win for any head coach anywhere?

Especially for Chizik, who couldn't go 5 feet without someone reminding him that he was 5-19 at Iowa State. And that was coming from Auburn fans.

This year, he's 12-0. Auburn's 12-0.

The biggest game? The biggest win?

You better believe it.

Read that again: Auburn was down 24-0 to Alabama in Tuscaloosa in front of 101,821, with its undefeated season on the line, and somehow it found a way.

Team of destiny? Ya think?

Now, it's on to the SEC championship game and South Carolina. One more win away from playing in the BCS national championship game.

Who saw that coming in August? Honestly?

Most people figured Auburn's Iron Bowl opponent would be playing the day after Thanksgiving for a shot at a national title.

Not the Tigers.

But finding a way is what this team's been all about. And the bigger the game, the better. Friday, it was the best.

"That was game that will certainly go down in history," Chizik said.

You better believe it.

Down 24-0 to Alabama on the road? In August, this game was over. On a blistery November afternoon, it was just getting started.

"What more could you ask for from a perfect scenario: 24 down to come back and win the game 28-27," said Auburn's senior middle linebacker Josh Bynes.

The truth is, you couldn't ask for anything more.

It's impossible. Not even if Auburn beat Alabama 36-0. Not even then.

No, this win, this way, with this team is the only way it could have gone down.

"Down 24-0 and you come back and win 28-27 against your rival?" Bynes asked rhetorically.

"Think about it. You really think we'll come back and win? No. And I think a lot of people thought that as well. And we came back and showed that we know how to finish games and go out with a victory."

And they don't come any bigger. Or with more on the line.

And now, they have to find one more.

Maybe Chizik was on to something by not saying this was the biggest win of his career.

He's still got more games to play.

The SEC championship game is next. Then, perhaps, the national championship.

They definitely don't come any bigger than that. ■

TOP RIGHT: Auburn Tigers Antoine Carter (45), Nick Fairley (90), and T'Sharvan Bell (22) celebrate after Fairley recovered an Alabama fumble. VASHA HUNT/OPELIKA-AUBURN NEWS

BOTTOM RIGHT: Quarterback Cam Newton squeezes into the end zone behind the blocking of Mike Berry (66) as the Tigers claw back to within a field goal in the second half. VASHA HUNT/OPELIKA-AUBURN NEWS

OPPOSITE LEFT TOP: Cam Newton gets off a pass in the face of pressure from Alabama linebacker Courtney Upshaw. VASHA HUNT/OPELIKA-AUBURN NEWS

OPPOSITE LEFT BOTTOM: Auburn running back Michael Dyer turns the corner as Alabama safety Mark Barron closes in. VASHA HUNT/OPELIKA-AUBURN NEWS

OPPOSITE RIGHT: Auburn defensive end Nosa Eguae (94), safety Zac Etheridge (4), safety Mike McNeil (26) and linebacker Craig Stevens (46) stop Alabama running back Trent Richardson cold in the second half. VASHA HUNT/OPELIKA-AUBURN NEWS

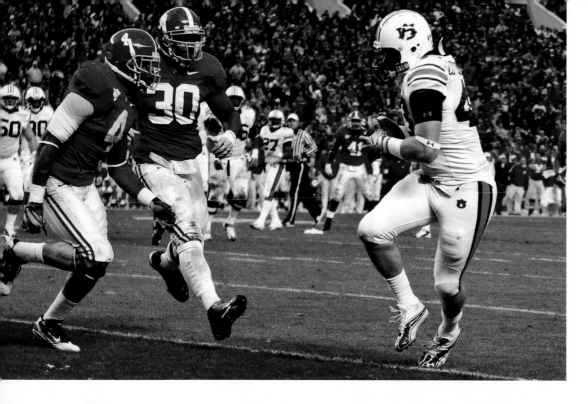

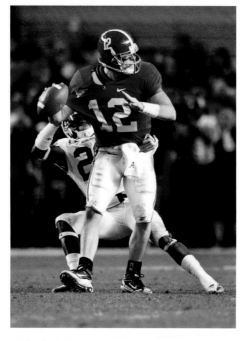

ABOVE: Alabama quarterback Greg McElroy (12) is helped off the field after being sacked by Auburn defensive back T'Sharvan Bell late in the game. VASHA HUNT/OPELIKA-AUBURN NEWS

TOP LEFT: Auburn tight end Philip Lutzenkirchen (43) makes the game-winning touchdown catch right at the goal line. VASHA HUNT/OPELIKA-AUBURN NEWS

BOTTOM LEFT: Philip Lutzenkirchen celebrates after making the game-winning catch. VASHA HUNT/OPELIKA-AUBURN NEWS

BOTTOM RIGHT: Auburn defensive back T'Sharvan Bell (22) sacks Alabama quarterback Greg McElroy (12). VASHA HUNT/OPELIKA-AUBURN NEWS

OPPOSITE: Auburn quarterback Cam Newton (2) makes one of the biggest plays of the game, going over the top for the one yard needed on a 4th and 1 deep in Auburn's territory. VASHA HUNT/OPELIKA-AUBURN NEWS

ABOVE: Auburn defensive lineman Nick Fairley looks to the sky after Alabama's failed pass attempt on 4th and long in the final minute.
VASHA HUNT/OPELIKA-AUBURN NEWS

RIGHT: Auburn defensive back Neiko Thorpe (15) signals to the fans after defending on Alabama's failed pass attempt on 4th and long in the final minute of the game. VASHA HUNT/OPELIKA-AUBURN NEWS

ABOVE: Auburn quarterback Cam Newton gives the 'oh no they didn't' sign after the game.
VASHA HUNT/OPELIKA-AUBURN NEWS

LEFT: Auburn defensive back T'Sharvan Bell celebrates with the fans after the game.
VASHA HUNT/OPELIKA-AUBURN NEWS

BELOW: Auburn Head Coach Gene Chizik talks with the press after the game.
VASHA HUNT/OPELIKA-AUBURN NEWS

²Auburn vs. ¹⁸South Carolina

SEC Championship, December 4, 2010 • Atlanta, Georgia • W 56-17

Newton leads Auburn to BCS Championship Game

By David Morrison | Staff Writer

ATLANTA -- Gene Chizik didn't need any qualifiers Saturday night.

No hemming and hawing. No "I haven't seen everybody in the nation" or "he's one of the best."

When the Auburn coach was asked whether he'd ever seen a player like Cam Newton after the top-ranked Tigers' 56-17 demolition of South Carolina in the SEC Championship Game, he didn't have to hesitate.

"No," Chizik said. "It's that simple. No. If you look over a 13-game span, I've never seen anything like it to be honest with you.

"He's probably the best football player I've ever seen."

Newton added another brushstroke to his masterpiece of a season in front of 75,802 fans at the Georgia Dome, accounting for 408 yards and six touchdowns against No. 19 South Carolina (9-4).

The title game MVP completed 17-of-28 passes for 335 yards and four scores, besting his high against an SEC team in the first half alone.

He ran 14 times for 73 yards and two more touchdowns, with his six scores tying Florida's Danny Wuerffel's 1996 performance for the most touchdowns in an SEC title game.

Auburn (13-0) set or tied eight championship game records Saturday, including the record for the most lopsided win in the game's 19-year history.

"When they tried to tackle me, for a player, I'm really honestly scared to get tackled, so my defense mechanism went up and I just didn't want to hit the ground," said Newton, who was available to the media for the first time in three weeks. "And I closed my eyes and squinched it, and when I opened them I still wasn't down, so I tried to find an open receiver."

Newton passed for 281 yards in the first half, with an especially exciting final 51.

With 7 seconds left in the half, the quarterback eluded a rusher, rolled right to the sideline and slung a pass toward the end zone and about six bodies.

It just so happened that the one who caught it was wearing white: Darvin Adams, who caught it at the whistle to send Auburn into the break up 28-14.

Adams broke an SEC title game record for receiving yards with 217 – all in the first half – on seven catches with two touchdowns.

Auburn scored on a Newton touchdown plunge after a South Carolina field goal to go up 21 points, then T'Sharvan Bell delivered the knockout blow on the next drive.

With a little help from Craig Stevens.

Stevens came free on a third-down blitz up the middle and forced Gamecocks quarterback Stephen Garcia into a hurry throw, one that was nearly hand-delivered to a waiting Bell, who took it 10 yards for the score.

"It just kind of fell right in my hands," Bell said. "Coach told Craig he'd have a big gap to run through. At the time it really didn't click with me. But he ran through there, he got his hand up and the ball just dropped right in my hands."

Any worry about South Carolina being ready for the pace of Auburn's offense because it had seen it before — something offensive coordinator Gus Malzahn professed earlier in the week — was put to rest when the Tigers motored to 227 yards in the first quarter and a record 589 yards for the game.

"We kind of got some momentum," Malzahn said. "Got in a good rhythm."

The last 20 minutes were little more than a formality for the Tigers, as they began running out the clock in the third quarter and pulled their starters about halfway through the fourth.

A group of them even lifted Newton on their shoulders and carried him onto the field as South Carolina was about to run its last play, forcing them to carry him back to the sidelines.

"When they told me they wanted to put me on their shoulders, I thought it was a joke at first," Newton said. "But as I went up in the air, it hit a part of my heart

ABOVE: Auburn quarterback Cam Newton greets the fans during TigerWalk before the Auburn-South Carolina SEC Championship game in Atlanta, Ga. VASHA HUNT/OPELIKA-AUBURN NEWS

LEFT: Cam Newton smiles as he runs from South Carolina's Devin Taylor. CLIFF WILLIAMS/OPELIKA-AUBURN NEWS

that I will never take away."

It must have been a welcome change for Newton, who's been putting the team on his back all season.

Even through the trials and tribulations of the NCAA investigation into his recruitment, to which Chizik maintained his policy of "no commenting" Saturday.

"As I said before, I've done nothing wrong," Newton read off a sheet of paper at the press conference. "I'm only going to answer questions about football in this game. So I ask that you please respect that, and thank you so much."

When Newton was asked whether his father — whose access to the program was "limited" by the NCAA ruling — could attend the Heisman ceremony, Chizik stepped in and said,

"We're going to stay away from those questions right now and stay football related, please, with all due respect."

Newton is eligible, a Heisman trophy candidate and one of the big reasons Auburn is celebrating its first SEC title since 2004 and a shot at Oregon in the BCS National Championship Game.

That's all there is for now.

"I just been living the dream this whole year I've just been living the dream, and I thank God for putting people in my life that has my best interests," Newton said. "And I can't stress it enough how blessed I truly am.

"And I just thank the people that's in my corner." ■

RIGHT: Aubie leads the team out before the SEC Championship game.
CLIFF WILLIAMS/OPELIKA-AUBURN NEWS

OPPOSITE: Auburn's Michael Dyer tries to break free of South Carolina's Antonio Allen (26) in the first half. CLIFF WILLIAMS/OPELIKA-AUBURN NEWS

ABOVE: Auburn's Darvin Adams catches a touchdown pass in the first half.
CLIFF WILLIAMS/OPELIKA-AUBURN NEWS

ABOVE RIGHT: Darvin Adams breaks from South Carolina's Stephon Gilmore for a touchdown in the first half. CLIFF WILLIAMS/OPELIKA-AUBURN NEWS

RIGHT: Auburn's Emory Blake reaches for South Carolina's Bryce Sherman during a kick return. CLIFF WILLIAMS/OPELIKA-AUBURN NEWS

ABOVE: Auburn quarterback Cam Newton plays to the crowd after his first touchdown pass during the first half. VASHA HUNT/OPELIKA-AUBURN NEWS

LEFT: Cam Newton throws downfield during the first half. VASHA HUNT/OPELIKA-AUBURN NEWS

BELOW: Auburn running back Onterio McCalebb scores the second Tiger touchdown, diving around South Carolina cornerback Stephon Gilmore. VASHA HUNT/OPELIKA-AUBURN NEWS

LEFT: Auburn's Nick Fairley is unable to block a South Carolina kick in the first half. CLIFF WILLIAMS/OPELIKA-AUBURN NEWS

BELOW LEFT: Auburn's Emory Blake is brought down by his face mask by South Carolina's D.J. Swearinger in the first half. CLIFF WILLIAMS/OPELIKA-AUBURN NEWS

OPPOSITE: Auburn celebrates the touchdown by running back Onterio McCalebb (23). VASHA HUNT/OPELIKA-AUBURN NEWS

BELOW: Auburn's Eric Smith looks to make a move on South Carolina strong safety DeVonte Holloman. CLIFF WILLIAMS/OPELIKA-AUBURN NEWS

ABOVE: Auburn running back Michael Dyer (5) makes a cut to avoid Carolina strong safety DeVonte Holloman. VASHA HUNT/OPELIKA-AUBURN NEWS

ABOVE RIGHT: Auburn Head Coach Gene Chizik argues with the refs during the first half. VASHA HUNT/OPELIKA-AUBURN NEWS

RIGHT: Cam Newton stretches for the end zone to score Auburn's the third touchdown of the first quarter. VASHA HUNT/OPELIKA-AUBURN NEWS

Adams shows up big on receiving end

Joe McAdory | Staff Writer

ATLANTA – "When he threw it, I said, 'Oh God, what's going to happen?'"

Darvin Adams answered South Carolina coach Steve Spurrier's question.

Adams, the junior Auburn wide receiver, grabbed a tipped pass in the end zone to score on a 51-yard Hail Mary pass from quarterback Cam Newton on the last play of the first half to give the Tigers a 28-14 lead and stick a knife in the Gamecocks' new-found momentum.

"I thought (Terrell Zachary) or Kodi (Burns) was going to catch the ball," said Adams, who set an SEC Championship game record Saturday with 217 receiving yards.

With the final seconds of the half ticking off the clock, Newton was flushed out of the pocket and rolled to his right. Chased by South Carolina defenders, Newton let the ball fly from the Tigers 45. The tight spiral was tipped by South Carolina safety DeVonte Holloman near the goal line.

Instead of crashing the ball to the Georgia Dome turf, Holloman's tip sent the ball upward into the end zone, floating in the direction of Adams.

"No. 5 (South Carolina cornerback Stephon Gilmore) tried to get it and I just went on top and got the ball," Adams said. "I was in the end zone and I saw the ball tipped in the air."

Just like that, the wind was gone from South Carolina's sails, though Spurrier didn't believe the play had an impact on the final outcome.

"We lost by, what, 35 points?," Spurrier said. "So, anyway, that was just one thing. That didn't cost us the game."

South Carolina scored seconds earlier to trim Auburn's lead to 21-14 when Stephen Garcia hit sophomore receiver Alshon Jeffery in the end zone on a 1-yard touchdown pass with 16 seconds left in the first half.

Momentum, Gamecocks.

Auburn used two plays to break the Gamecocks' hearts with Adams' magical reception and waltzed into the locker room with a two-touchdown advantage.

Momentum, Tigers.

"I thought that was a huge turning point in the game," Auburn head coach Gene Chizik said. "The only way we were going to do that is if we felt like position field-wise, we could take one shot, try to eat up 10, 12 yards and get in range where Cam could throw it."

South Carolina kicker Spencer Lanning helped set the Tigers in good field position when he didn't follow his coach's orders on the kickoff following Jeffery's touchdown.

"That was a communication breakdown," Spurrier explained. "We told him to kick a line drive and he decides to kick a one-hopper. But he told me he was trying to kick a line drive."

Auburn's Eric Smith fielded the ball at the 30 and returned it to the 41. An 8-yard sideline route to Adams moved the chains to the 49 with time for one more play.

"We took one shot," Chizik said. "We knew Cameron could throw the ball 70 yards in the air or whatever the case may have been at that point. He's done it in practice. So, we said, 'let's throw that up and see if we can't get a big play out of it.'"

Newton agreed.

"We've been in that situation before in practice and repetition is the key to success," Newton said. "When the time came for us to make a play for that, Darvin did an excellent job."

The touchdown reception was Adams' seventh — and final catch — on a record-breaking afternoon.

"Darvin is the definition of a complete football player," Newton said. "He blocks. He catches."

"Whatever coach asks him to do, he's willing to do it. And that just goes to show you what he did today, just the little things that we see every day out of Darvin Adams." ∎

ABOVE: Auburn wide receiver Darvin Adams (89) high-fives Auburn wide receiver Kodi Burns (18) after Adams' hail-mary touchdown reception. VASHA HUNT/OPELIKA-AUBURN NEWS

LEFT: Darvin Adams hauls in the Cam Newton 51-yard hail-mary touchdown pass on the final play of the first half. VASHA HUNT/OPELIKA-AUBURN NEWS

LEFT: Auburn's Emory Blake catches a touchdown pass from Cam Newton in front of South Carolina's Akeem Auguste. CLIFF WILLIAMS/OPELIKA-AUBURN NEWS

BELOW LEFT: Emory Blake and Terrell Zachery celebrate following a Blake touchdown. CLIFF WILLIAMS/OPELIKA-AUBURN NEWS

OPPOSITE ABOVE LEFT: Auburn's Michael Dyer runs against South Carolina in the 4th quarter. CLIFF WILLIAMS/OPELIKA-AUBURN NEWS

OPPOSITE BELOW LEFT: Auburn's Kodi Burns tries to break the tackle of South Carolina's Damario Jeffery in the 4th quarter. CLIFF WILLIAMS/OPELIKA-AUBURN NEWS

OPPOSITE RIGHT: Cam Newton celebrates at the start of the 4th quarter. CLIFF WILLIAMS/OPELIKA-AUBURN NEWS

BELOW: Auburn running back Onterio McCalebb gets loose in the South Carolina secondary. VASHA HUNT/OPELIKA-AUBURN NEWS

LEFT: Auburn wide receiver Emory Blake (80) catches a touchdown pass during the second half. VASHA HUNT/OPELIKA-AUBURN NEWS

OPPOSITE: Auburn running back Michael Dyer (5) makes a strong cut to head upfield. VASHA HUNT/OPELIKA-AUBURN NEWS

ABOVE: Auburn coach Gene Chizik meets with Fiesta Bowl officials following a win over South Carolina. CLIFF WILLIAMS/OPELIKA-AUBURN NEWS

LEFT: Auburn quarterback Barrett Trotter (14) gets work in the second half. VASHA HUNT/OPELIKA-AUBURN NEWS

Tigers get opportunity 2004 team never had

By David Morrison | Staff Writer

ATLANTA -- The tunnel to the locker room provided an oasis of calm from the chaos on the field after Auburn's 56-17 thrashing of South Carolina in the SEC Championship Game.

That is, until Tigers cornerback T'Sharvan Bell skipped in, waving an orange shaker, the sound of his voice resonating off the walls by the locker room.

"They never gave us a chance, baby," Bell said. "That's what makes it so sweet."

Bell and the rest of the Tigers got the confetti bath — which they soon turned into an arena for sprawling on the ground and making confetti angels — the posed pictures with the wooden championship trophy and the hats telling the world who the 2010 SEC champions are.

For seniors like Josh Bynes, ones who were there for 5-7, it couldn't have been much sweeter.

"It's a blessing to have this opportunity," Bynes said. "Emotionally it's all over the place. You want to cry, you want to celebrate, you want to do all kinds of things.

"We expected this. If we did what we were supposed to do on the field all 12 games prior to this, then come into this game and dominate, we knew we were going to be SEC champions."

It was, as Bell implied, an unlikely scenario for the Tigers at the beginning of the year, one that became more and more likely as the weeks went by and they kept finding ways to win.

But the Tigers didn't need any late-game heroics or implausible comebacks in this one. The celebration started about halfway through the third quarter.

"It shows the resiliency of Auburn men and how Gene (Chizik) and his staff got these guys to buy in," athletics director Jay Jacobs said. "It's an ascension that's come along quicker than anyone ever saw. Thirteen-and-0 is amazing in itself, but to do it two years after our team won just five games is a miracle."

With its SEC title, the 2010 version of the Tigers have an opportunity to play for the national championship, something the other 13-0 Auburn team – 2004 – didn't get.

"We talked about it all year and we got here. The question was what we were going to do," defensive end Antoine Carter said. "We got here and won. It's a great feeling for everybody.

"I'm in the now right now. I'll focus more on Glendale tomorrow when I wake up."

No. 2 Oregon awaits in Glendale, Ariz., on Jan. 10 for the national title, another team with no shortage of offensive firepower.

Tigers' offensive coordinator Gus Malzahn is a man who likes pace in his offense.
Predictably, he likes Oregon.

"I have a lot of respect for (Ducks coach) Chip Kelly. He's a great coach," the Tigers' offensive coordinator said. "I love how fast they play."

About as fast as Auburn?

"I don't know," Malzahn said. "The night I saw, they were getting it pretty good." ■

ABOVE: Auburn quarterback Cameron Newton makes a snow angel in the confetti after the SEC championship win. VASHA HUNT/OPELIKA-AUBURN NEWS

OPPOSITE: Cam Newton is carried on the shoulders of his team mates following the win over South Carolina.
CLIFF WILLIAMS/OPELIKA-AUBURN NEWS

ABOVE: The Auburn football team celebrates following a 56-17 win over South Carolina.
CLIFF WILLIAMS/OPELIKA-AUBURN NEWS

ABOVE LEFT: Cam Newton embraces Auburn Head Coach Gene Chizik. VASHA HUNT/OPELIKA-AUBURN NEWS

LEFT: Cam Newton slaps the hands of adoring fans.
CLIFF WILLIAMS/OPELIKA-AUBURN NEWS

FAR LEFT: Auburn defensive end Corey Lemonier (55), Auburn defensive end Nosa Eguae (94) and Auburn defensive back Dee Ford (95) celebrate in the stands after winning the SEC Championship. The Tigers face Oregon in the BCS Championship in Glendale, Ariz.
VASHA HUNT/OPELIKA-AUBURN NEWS

ABOVE: Auburn fans line the entrance to the Best Buy Theater in Times Square on Dec. 11 for a Tiger Walk, New York style.
MIKE SZVETITZ/OPELIKA-AUBURN NEWS

RIGHT & BELOW: Opelika-Auburn News front pages report Cam Newton's Heisman triumph.

OPPOSITE: Auburn quarterback Cam Newton answers questions from the media on Friday, Dec. 10, in New York. MIKE SZVETITZ/OPELIKA-AUBURN NEWS

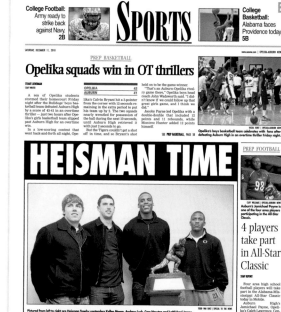

AU HOOPS:
Rutgers tops Tigers in SEC-Big East Invite.
7B

SPORTS

FOOTBALL:
Gators hire new head coach.
7B

SUNDAY, DECEMBER 12, 2010

www.oanow.com | OPELIKA-AUBURN NEWS

2010 HEISMAN TROPHY

IT'S A LANDSLIDE

AU's Newton wins Heisman Trophy by wide margin

Auburn quarterback Cam Newton poses with the Heisman Trophy on Saturday in New York. Newton became just the third player in Auburn history to win the prestigious award.

TODD J. VAN EMST | SPECIAL TO THE NEWS

Newton becomes school's 3rd player to win honor

DAVID MORRISON
STAFF WRITER

NEW YORK — When he heard his name called, it took Cam Newton only three enormous strides to make up the

Heisman Trophy on Saturday night at the Best Buy Theater just off Times Square, following in the footsteps of Pat Sullivan (1971) and Bo Jackson (1985), who was at the Heisman ceremony for the first

records at your school and account for 49 touchdowns and 4,040 yards from scrimmage on the No. 1 team in the nation.

"There is no question that Cameron is highly deserving of the most prestigious honor

Newton deserves 'thank yous,' too

NEW YORK — Since his name first came up in the Heisman Trophy race, Cam Newton has been very vocal about where he thinks the focus should and shouldn't be. Less of him, more of his

bound, but without his teammates, he's not in New York City this weekend with a chance to

Cam Wins the Heisman

Newton wins Heisman in landslide victory

David Morrison | Staff Writer

NEW YORK – Mary Kathryn Papaioannou should have been studying for finals.

Instead, the New York University law school student – also a Birmingham native with an undergraduate degree from Auburn – stood with about 1,000 other Tiger fans outside the Best Buy Theater on Saturday night, breaking the news that wouldn't be official until about three hours later.

Cam Newton is the 2010 Heisman Trophy winner.

"The university sent shakers, I started making posters and signs when I should have been studying," said Papaioannou, a member of the New York Auburn Club.

"I can study after the Heisman ceremony."

The junior quarterback became the third player in Auburn history to win the Heisman, receiving 729 first-place votes and 2,263 points, the sixth-highest point total in Heisman history counting USC running back Reggie Bush's vacated results.

The embattled quarterback – who's been hounded for the past five weeks by allegations of a pay-for-play plan during his recruitment last year – needed a moment to gather himself during his acceptance speech, with former winners on the stage behind him, telling him "take your time, deep breaths."

"Thank you to the Auburn Family, for all the support you've given me during these trying times," Newton said.

Stanford quarterback Andrew Luck finished second (1,079 points) in the voting, Oregon running back LaMichael James finished third (916 points) and Boise State quarterback Kellen Moore finished fourth (635 points).

Newton's 1,184-point margin over Luck is the 11th-highest in Heisman history.

The 6-foot-6, 250-pound Newton accounted for a school-record 49 touchdowns and more than 4,000 yards from scrimmage this year, also becoming the first player in SEC history to rush for 1,000 yards and throw for 2,000 in the same season and the second player in NCAA history to run and pass for 20 touchdowns in the same year.

Newton is the first Auburn player to win the Maxwell and O'Brien awards, and the third Tiger – after Pat Sullivan (1971) and Bo Jackson (1985) – to win the Walter Camp Player of the Year Award.

And Saturday night, Newton joined Sullivan and Jackson in the Heisman fraternity.

"This is a phenomenal young man," Auburn coach Gene Chizik said. "He's different on the field and he's different off the field. He's a great kid. We get much joy and much satisfaction out of seeing our own get the benefits and see the fruits of his labor, which are many. It's very well deserved, no question about it.

"Everything he gets he's worked for and he deserves every bit of it." ∎

Fan Shots

We asked our readers to submit their best Auburn football photos and the response was amazing! More than 1,000 photos were submitted. Here's a selection of some of our favorites!

1: Garrison and Justin are ALL IN with the Tigers as they take on the Georgia Bulldogs at Jordan-Hare Stadium. (PHOTO BY TAMMALA BROOKS) **2:** The girls in their Auburn dresses before South Carolina (PHOTO BY HANNAH MCCORD) **3:** Cole Breedlove Age 3. (PHOTO BY CATINA BREEDLOVE) **4:** Toomer's Corner was still rocking at 3 a.m. and the O-A News was in full display! (PHOTO BY JIMMY RHYNE) **5:** Brian Cole and daughter Caroline with Aubie during A-Day festivities. (PHOTO BY AMY COLE) **6:** Laney Caroline Payne of Valley, 2 years old at the Georgia game. Daughter of Brandee and Chase Payne (PHOTO BY CHASE PAYNE) **7:** Stephen Amason and Onterio (PHOTO BY JANEEN)

1: Seth Granberry "AUnicycle Man" jumping rope on his unicycle before Tiger Walk. (PHOTO BY SETH GRANBERRY) **2:** Celebrating with our sign after our win against Clemson in blue! (PHOTO BY NATALIE SALTER) **3:** Stephanie and Joshua Graham take a break from their wedding reception to celebrate Cam's Heisman win. (PHOTO BY THOMAS BOUTWELL) **4:** Zachary and Lee waiting for some TV time. (PHOTO BY APRIL NEWMAN) **5:** Wave at the Clemson game (PHOTO BY NICKEY JACKSON) **6:** An Auburn cheerleader runs the flag after another Tiger score. (PHOTO BY KENNY SMITH) **7:** Pre-game panorama of the Georgia Dome for the SEC Championship Game. (PHOTO BY MARTIN PIERCE IV) **8:** DeAngelo takes time to say hello to fan pre-game (PHOTO BY WALTER MAULDIN) **9:** Toomer's Corner after the Auburn Tigers' defeated Oregon to bring home a national championship. (PHOTO BY CHRIS ARNOLD)

1: Debbie Sutton and Kayla Roberts waiting for game time. (PHOTO BY DEBRA SUTTON) **2:** Marley and the Auburn cheerleaders. (PHOTO BY ELIZABETH PHILLIPS) **3:** Amy Cole with Mr. Penny celebrating at Toomer's Corner after the SEC Championship Game. (PHOTO BY AMY COLE) **4:** 3 days before Bama Game, Cam said "We are ready!" (PHOTO BY WALTER MAULDIN) **5:** Orange and blue even in the skies. (PHOTO BY NICKEY JACKSON) **6:** The band leading us in "It's Great to be an Auburn Tiger!" (PHOTO BY LEA HOWELL) **7:** Chris Johnston's and Joey Vicker's ultimate tailgate 3 table flip-cup game! Auburn fans on left, Clemson on the right. (PHOTO BY CHRIS JOHNSTON) **8:** Maryn Kate Davis meeting Coach Pat Dye! (PHOTO BY JANA DAVIS)

1: Madison, Gabriel, Danna, Jeremy, Omar, and Tristian showing team spirit before Tiger Walk starts. (PHOTO BY DANNA SAIA) **2:** I'm one of Auburn's biggest fans. They call me "Mr. Auburn Bicycle Man." Me and my Tigers go to every home game. (PHOTO BY JOE DUNN) **3:** After the LSU game. (PHOTO BY AMY HAYNES) **4:** Connor & Antonio visiting Santa. (PHOTO BY CATHY TROHA GRASSI) **5:** Charlie hanging out with the 'pretty girls' at the Library Tailgate Party. (PHOTO BY MIA CAREY) **6:** Celebrating Auburn's win over Alabama at Toomers Corner with the Auburn family and my family. Hal, Lauren, and Ryan Smith. (PHOTO BY HAL SMITH) **7:** April and Patrick Coulter pose next to Bo Jackson's uniform in the AU locker room after the AU-Chattanooga game. (PHOTO BY APRIL COULTER) **8:** A panoramic shot of Toomer's Corner after the game against the Arkansas Razorbacks. (PHOTO BY BENJAMIN MEADS)

121

1: Ready to go beat those Georgia Dawgs! (PHOTO BY JIM MCCRORY) **2:** Anna and I with our favorite band member before the Iron Bowl began. (PHOTO BY NATALIE SALTER) **3:** Kinzlee waving the Trooper Towel yelling WAR EAGLE! (PHOTO BY ANGEL GROVES) **4:** Terri's Auburn petits fours. (PHOTO BY NANCY FIELDS) **5:** CAM NEWTON! (PHOTO BY TABITHA PRELSEY) **6:** Toomer's after winning the 2010 SEC Championship Game. (PHOTO BY BOBBY BOND) **7:** Friends at a tailgate party. (PHOTO BY DANNA SAIA) **8:** Fan taking a picture of Aubie. (PHOTO BY NICKEY JACKSON)

1: An up close panoramic photo taken from Toomer's Corner after the game against the Arkansas Razorbacks. (PHOTO BY BENJAMIN MEADS) **2:** Die hard fans celebrating the big win over Georgia. It was the perfect last home game of an undefeated season! (PHOTO BY CASEY MARTIN) **3:** Alison Hall and Bridget Wingo are ALL IN for the Auburn vs. Georgia game. (PHOTO BY ALISON HALL) **4:** Tiger Walk - First Game of the Season. (PHOTO BY CRYSTAL RUSSELL) **5:** Students celebrating after Auburn wins SEC Championship. (PHOTO BY DREW SMITH) **6:** Tate Olsen, 1, shows his support on Halloween Weekend. (PHOTO BY KARA OLSEN) **7:** Jack and Will Whittenburg playing in the toilet paper after the Georgia game. (PHOTO BY AMY WHITTENBURG) **8:** The famous "YES WE CAM" poster. (PHOTO BY EMILY MCBRIDE)

¹Auburn vs. ²Oregon

BCS Championship, January 10, 2011 • Glendale, Ariz. • W 22-19

Dyer leads offense, Tigers to title-game win

David Morrison | Staff Writer

GLENDALE, Ariz. — Mike Dyer felt nearly every part of his body hit the ground but the important ones, rolled over Oregon's Eddie Pleasant and heard thousands of voices.

All telling him to keep on running.

"I kind of figured my knee wasn't down. I didn't hear no whistle," Dyer said. "Even the crowd was saying, 'Go! Go!'"

Dyer got back to his feet and ran 37 yards down to the Oregon 23, turning in one of those plays that will be talked about for years to come in Auburn.

It was that play — and a 16-yard run that followed — that set up Wes Byrum's 19-yard, game-winning field goal at the buzzer to deliver Auburn a 22-19 win over Oregon in front of a record 78,603 fans at the BCS National Championship Game at University of Phoenix Stadium on Monday night.

It was the Tigers' first national championship in 53 years.

"We said that we wanted to go from good to great," head coach Gene Chizik said. "And I can sit here tonight and I can tell you that the Auburn Tigers are the best football team in the United States."

No. 1 Auburn (14-0) took over at its 26-yard line with 2:33 to go, after a 2-yard shovel pass from Darron Thomas to LaMichael James and a 2-point pass from James to Jeff Maehl — one in which Maehl made a jumping catch in the back of the end zone — knotted the game at 19.

One of the rarest of all occurrences this season, a lost fumble by Cam Newton, set up the tying drive for No.

2 Oregon (12-1).

Newton finished with 265 yards, two touchdowns and an interception on 20-of-34 passing, also running 22 times for 64 yards and only his second lost fumble of the year.

"I said 'We're going to go down and score,'" offensive coordinator Gus Malzahn said. "They've done that all year. They found a way.

"Michael Dyer made one of those unbelievable runs that people in Auburn will remember forever, and helped us win the game."

Newton started off the drive with a 15-yard pass to Emory Blake, then Dyer took an inside draw and appeared to go down after a 5-yard gain.

But none of the vital areas touched the ground, allowing him to scamper for 32 more. And a replay review upheld the call.

"He's got great balance," Malzahn said. "He's one of those guys that spins around."

It was a bizarre signature play for a bizarre championship game, one that included Oregon getting stuffed on a fourth-and-goal from the 1 but converting a fourth-and-8 with a fake punt; Auburn giving up 449 yards but only 19 points; and both teams going scoreless in the first quarter of a game that was supposed to be an epic shootout.

The two teams combined for 968 yards on the night but a pedestrian 41 points.

Defensive coordinator Ted Roof said all the predictions of a high-scoring game in the lead-up to Monday might have swayed his unit's play.

"I hope so," Roof said. "I think it may have."

Oregon went up first on a field goal, then Auburn answered with a 35-yard pass from Newton to Kodi Burns.

The Ducks went back up on a pass to James — followed by an option to kicker Rob Beard for the 2-point conversion — then a Mike Blanc safety and a 30-yard

pass from Newton to Blake put Auburn back up.

A 28-yard Byrum field goal gave Auburn an apparently stable 19-11 lead, especially with the way the Tigers were running the ball.

Until Newton's fumble.

Another fourth-down conversion and eight plays later, the Ducks had a tie game.

Then it was time for Dyer, the offensive MVP after finishing with 143 yards on 22 carries, to take over.

"There's a lot of things that happened this year that

ABOVE: The Auburn faithful gather to cheer for the Tigers during the pep rally held at The Fiesta in Scottsdale, Ariz. It was the last major event before the BCS National Championship Game. Aubie, the AU Cheerleaders and Mr. Penny all pitched in to help lead the crowd, and Terry Henley, AU '73 Alabama Sports Hall of Famer, MC'd the event.
VASHA HUNT/OPELIKA-AUBURN NEWS

OPPOSITE: Auburn running back Michael Dyer (5) breaks loose for a big run after Oregon thought he was down on the final drive of the game.
VASHA HUNT/OPELIKA-AUBURN NEWS

I never really expected," Dyer said. "I'm just glad to be here with my team. Glad to be a part of this."

Dyer picked up another 16 yards on another draw down to the 1 — after a review reversed a touchdown call — two plays later, and Byrum did the rest.

It was the senior's 60th field goal at Auburn, his sixth game-winner in his college career and his third this season after hitting ones against Clemson and Kentucky.

He celebrated a bit more after this one than his subdued fist pump against the Wildcats. Then again, he didn't get a hug and proclamation of "You're the best kicker to ever play here" from Al Del Greco after he beat Kentucky.

"It's an unbelievable experience, especially after the career he had at Auburn," Byrum said. "It's an unbelievable thing."

There wasn't much about Auburn's season that wasn't unbelievable.

"We're the champions," safety Zac Etheridge said. "That's all I need to say." ∎

ABOVE RIGHT: Aubie and the AU Cheerleaders lead the crowd in a cheer as Auburn fans gather to support the Tigers during the pep rally held at The Fiesta in Scottsdale, Ariz. VASHA HUNT/OPELIKA-AUBURN NEWS

BOTTOM RIGHT: The Auburn faithful cheer for the Tigers during the pep rally held at The Fiesta in Scottsdale, Ariz. VASHA HUNT/OPELIKA-AUBURN NEWS

ABOVE: Auburn's Gus Malzahn gathers his troops during the first half. VASHA HUNT/OPELIKA-AUBURN NEWS

ABOVE LEFT: Auburn graduate student Jordan Brewer of Alexander City, Ala. cheers at the SkyBar in downtown Auburn during the first half of the BCS Championship Game between Auburn and Oregon. CLIFF WILLIAMS/OPELIKA-AUBURN NEWS

LEFT: Auburn quarterback Cameron Newton (2) warms up during pre-game festivities. VASHA HUNT/OPELIKA-AUBURN NEWS

Auburn's defense negates Oregon's speed

Mike Szvetitz | Staff Writer

GLENDALE, Ariz. — Defense wins championships. Even ones that give up 449 yards of offense.

But that stat won't be remembered as much as Auburn's first BCS title.

And the Tigers did it with defense.

Auburn limited the nation's No. 1 scoring offense to just 19 points Monday night at University of Phoenix Stadium, coming up big time after time, including a safety, two turnovers and a goal-line stand.

"I'm just so proud of our kids," Auburn defensive coordinator Ted Roof said. "But tonight was just kind of how we've done it all year.

"What happens in games like this, guys rise above things and make great plays. And they did."

Billed as an offensive shootout, with the Ducks boasting mythical speed and offensive numbers, the Tigers' defense came in with a chip on its shoulder.

"About five weeks ago, we challenged our defense, and I think they had about all they wanted to hear about the speed and tempo," Auburn head coach Gene Chizik said following the game. "Our defense was focused for one month. They went out and practiced every day to win a national championship — every day.

"You talk about the word 'respond.' They responded today. One of the reasons we will be able to wear that ring is because of how well they played."

Josh Bynes, especially, had enough of the "offensive" talk.

"Yeah, defense wins championships," he said on the field just minutes after the end of the game, confetti still showering down. "It showed definitely in this

---

RIGHT: Auburn defensive end Nosa Eguae (94) and Auburn defensive lineman Mike Blanc (93) celebrate a defensive stop to start the game.
VASHA HUNT/OPELIKA-AUBURN NEWS

OPPOSITE: A host of Tigers stop Oregon running back Kenjon Barner (24) on a kick return. VASHA HUNT/OPELIKA-AUBURN NEWS

game. It wasn't going to be a high, 50-48, 99-98 kind of game.

"We pulled through. We held Oregon's offense, because we knew how to be physical. ... Physicality beats speed any day."

Roof was still trying to put his feelings into words when asked about them.

"Really a sense of relief and a sense of pride for our kids and the Auburn family," the defensive coordinator said. "Of course, it hasn't sunk in yet, but we won

another game. And it happened to be a really, really big one."

His defense was a big part of that.

"Man, our defense, we showed America everything we done each and every Saturday out there on the field," said Nick Fairley, Auburn's junior defensive tackle and the national championship game's defensive MVP. "We have been doing this ... for 14 weeks. We just went unnoticed throughout the year. Now that we got noticed out here on the big stage, we just showed

what we can do."

Roof, however, doesn't want his squad to take all the credit.

"Teams win championships," he said. "It was a total team effort tonight against a really, really good football team." ∎

LEFT: Auburn quarterback Cam Newton rushed for 64 yards on 22 carries. VASHA HUNT/OPELIKA-AUBURN NEWS

OPPOSITE TOP LEFT: Auburn defensive back Demond Washington (14) makes the game's first interception. VASHA HUNT/OPELIKA-AUBURN NEWS

OPPOSITE TOP RIGHT: Auburn running back Onterio McCalebb (23) gets loose. VASHA HUNT/OPELIKA-AUBURN NEWS

OPPOSITE BOTTOM LEFT: Auburn Head Coach Gene Chizik paces the sidelines. VASHA HUNT/OPELIKA-AUBURN NEWS

OPPOSITE BOTTOM RIGHT: Auburn linebacker Josh Bynes (17) sets the defense. VASHA HUNT/OPELIKA-AUBURN NEWS

BELOW: Auburn wide receiver Kodi Burns (18) catches a pass and runs it in for the game's first TD. VASHA HUNT/OPELIKA-AUBURN NEWS

Big 2nd quarter helps lift Tigers

Mike Szvetitz | Staff Writer

GLENDALE, Ariz. — The second quarter started with Nick Fairley dropping Oregon quarterback Darron Thomas for a 6-yard loss.

It ended with Auburn running into the locker room with a 16-11 lead.

What happened in between laid the groundwork for Auburn's first BCS National Championship. Fairley's sack kept Oregon out of the end zone on a third-and-2 play from the 3, forcing the Ducks to settle for a 26-yard field goal and a 3-0 lead.

Then, it was all Auburn.

In the second quarter, the Tigers ran 36 plays for 258 yards, while Oregon ran just 11 plays for 107 yards, with 81 coming on one play — Thomas' pass to Jeff Maehl that set up the Ducks' first touchdown.

"That's what our offense is used to doing, helping out our defense a lot by keeping us off the field," senior defensive tackle Mike Blanc said. "I just feel like, defense and offense, we started a little slow, but offense came though. We knew that was going to happen."

Auburn quarterback Cam Newton started the game 0-for-2 with an interception, but in the second quarter he found his groove, completing 14-for-18 passes for 174 yards and two touchdowns.

After Fairley and the Tigers' defense held Oregon to a field goal to begin the second period, Newton led the offense on an eight-play, 82-yard scoring drive that finished with Kodi Burns catching his first touchdown of the year. That 35-yard grab put Auburn up 7-3 with 12:00 to play until halftime.

Oregon answered right back with a four-play, 93-yard drive that took just 57 seconds. Maehl's catch and run was the highlight, capped off by an 8-yard, throwback screen to LaMichael James for a score. Oregon's 2-point conversion was good for an 11-7 lead.

After that drive, however, the Ducks were grounded, gaining just 20 yards on six plays the rest of the quarter.

"That was one of the whole deals going in was to try and eliminate the home run balls," Auburn defensive coordinator Ted Roof said. "Because that's what happens if you watch them throughout the season, the game's even, even, even, then all of a sudden, boom,

they score three touchdowns. Then it gets out of hand.

"So our whole thing all night was, let's get lined up, let's be physical, let's play hard and let's keep the ball in the park and see what happens."

Then, it was the offense's turn.

Auburn had drives of eight, 16, six and six plays in the second 15 minutes.

The Tigers also had a safety, thanks to defensive lineman Mike Blanc's tackle for a loss on James in the end zone with 3:26 left.

"Before we went out there, coach was like, 'We need a big-time play, right now,'" Blanc said. "And in my mind, that thought was going through my head."

The safety was, ironically, set up by Auburn's offense. The Tigers went 16 plays down to the Ducks' 1, but Newton missed a wide open Eric Smith in the end zone, turning the ball over on downs.

Two plays later, Newton got it back and led the Tigers to their second touchdown drive, capping it with a 30-yard pass to Blake for a 16-11 lead. ∎

ABOVE: Oregon Head Coach Chip Kelly watches during the first half. VASHA HUNT/OPELIKA-AUBURN NEWS

LEFT: Auburn wide receiver Emory Blake (80) grabs a throw from Auburn quarterback Cameron Newton (2) for a TD in the second quarter.
VASHA HUNT/OPELIKA-AUBURN NEWS

FAR LEFT TOP: Oregon running back LaMichael James (21) celebrates a TD with Oregon offensive lineman Jordan Holmes (54).
VASHA HUNT/OPELIKA-AUBURN NEWS

FAR LEFT BOTTOM: Auburn wide receiver Terrell Zachery (81) drags a defender.
VASHA HUNT/OPELIKA-AUBURN NEWS

OPPOSITE: Auburn running back Michael Dyer (5) rushed for 143 yards.
VASHA HUNT/OPELIKA-AUBURN NEWS

133

RIGHT: Auburn defensive back Woody Parramore (48) and Auburn defensive back Daren Bates (25) chest bump Auburn defensive end Corey Lemonier (55) and Auburn defensive lineman Mike Blanc (93) after a fourth down stop deep in Auburn territory.
VASHA HUNT/OPELIKA-AUBURN NEWS

BOTTOM LEFT: Auburn Head Coach Gene Chizik locks in. VASHA HUNT/OPELIKA-AUBURN NEWS

BOTTOM RIGHT: Oregon wide receiver Lavasier Tuinei (80) drops a 3rd down pass in the fourth quarter. VASHA HUNT/OPELIKA-AUBURN NEWS

OPPOSITE: Auburn defensive back T'Sharvan Bell (22) plays to the crowd after a hard hit.
VASHA HUNT/OPELIKA-AUBURN NEWS

LEFT: Auburn running back Michael Dyer (5) breaks loose for a big run after Oregon thought he was down on the final drive of the game. VASHA HUNT/ OPELIKA-AUBURN NEWS

OPPOSITE TOP LEFT: Auburn quarterback Cameron Newton (2) throws downfield late in the game. VASHA HUNT/OPELIKA-AUBURN NEWS

OPPOSITE TOP RIGHT: Auburn quarterback Cameron Newton (2) plays through pain. VASHA HUNT/OPELIKA-AUBURN NEWS

OPPOSITE BOTTOM LEFT: Auburn linebacker Josh Bynes (17) revs the crowd. VASHA HUNT/OPELIKA-AUBURN NEWS

OPPOSITE BOTTOM RIGHT: Auburn quarterback Cameron Newton (2) gets loose late in the game. VASHA HUNT/OPELIKA-AUBURN NEWS

Kick makes Auburn a national champion for generation of hungry fans

Mike Szvetitz | Staff Writer

GLENDALE, Ariz. — A last-second field goal to win the national championship.

Would you want it any other way?

Not this year. Not this team. No way.

"Nah," Gus Malzahn said. "This is the way to do it, man."

And Auburn's been doing it this way all year, gnawing its nails down to the nub, all the way to its first BCS national championship.

The Tigers have trailed in nine out of their 14 games this season, only to come back and win them all. Monday wasn't their biggest deficit — trailing by 4 at most — but it was the most special.

And the most exciting.

Mike Dyer's 37-yard, "He did what?" run to put Auburn in field-goal range on the final, last-minute drive was just another example of just how special this team and its season has been.

Even when Dyer looked down, he wasn't. Just like the Tigers.

Team of destiny? There is no doubt.

Now, they're national champs. Forever.

"I wanted it to come down just like this to the wire," Auburn senior middle linebacker Josh Bynes said. "It's the most amazing feeling. And it's a feeling we had since spring last year. And to finally see that feeling come true, it's the most amazing thing that we could have in our whole life."

Philip Lutzenkirchen couldn't even think seconds after Wes Byrum blasted through his game-winning 19-yarder.

"I don't know what to say. I don't know what to say," he kept repeating. "We did it."

Good enough.

Good enough for a championship. Good enough for 14-0. Good enough for a generation of Auburn fans who have been waiting 53 years for this. A lifetime.

Now, a lifetime of memories.

Auburn is a national champion again.

"This is my dream," legendary Auburn coach Pat Dye said. "These kids lived my dream. All I could be was a fan and watch them do the magic. And I'm going to tell you, it was magic and magical and brilliant and guts and character and all of the adjectives that you can add to it to make it what it was."

What it was, was a team that refused to quit. A team that refused to give in. A team that refused to let anything get in its way. Not a 24-point lead. Not an NCAA investigation. Not off-the-field distractions. Nothing.

"Nobody believed us, but we believed in each other and believed in ourselves," Bynes said. "When everybody doubted Cam, when everybody doubted us and doubted the whole Auburn family, we showed the world. SEC Champs, national champs, baby. No. 1 in the world."

And when Byrum's field goal went through the uprights, the world according to Dye, Shug Jordan, Pat Sullivan, Bo Jackson, James Bostic, Carnell Williams and Ronnie Brown stopped.

"This is just … and all of us old timers and all the former players, the former coaches and the fans that have endured and withstood the heartaches that go with being there and not getting to hold that ball up there, this football team, this staff, they did it for us," Dye said after the trophy presentation. "I mean, they did for themselves, but we're going to bask in the glory."

The ghosts of 1983, 1993 and 2004 are gone. No more. This team, this year, exorcised them all.

This team, this year, this way.

"We're here," senior guard Mike Berry said. "We did it."

National champs.

Was there ever a doubt? ∎

ABOVE: Auburn kicker Wes Byrum (18) kicks the game-winning and national championship clinching field goal as time expires during the 2011 BCS National Championship Game. VASHA HUNT/OPELIKA-AUBURN NEWS

LEFT: Auburn quarterback Cam Newton does a lap for the fans after the 2011 BCS National Championship Game between Auburn and Oregon Monday, Jan. 10, 2011 in Glendale, Ariz.
VASHA HUNT/OPELIKA-AUBURN NEWS

FAR LEFT: Gus Malzahn celebrates after the 2011 BCS National Championship Game win. VASHA HUNT/OPELIKA-AUBURN NEWS

BOTTOM LEFT: Teammates mob kicker Wes Byrum after the senior's game-winning field goal. VASHA HUNT/OPELIKA-AUBURN NEWS

BOTTOM RIGHT: The Arizona Republic distributes Tigers Win! after the 2011 BCS National Championship Game.
VASHA HUNT/OPELIKA-AUBURN NEWS

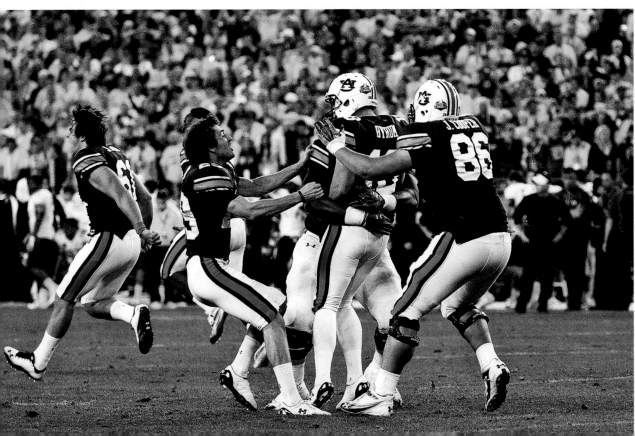

RIGHT: Erin Andrews interviews offensive MVP Auburn running back Michael Dyer (5) after the 2011 BCS National Championship Game. VASHA HUNT/OPELIKA-AUBURN NEWS

BOTTOM LEFT: Auburn defensive lineman Nick Fairley (90) and Auburn running back Michael Dyer (5) celebrate their MVP awards after the 2011 BCS National Championship Game. VASHA HUNT/OPELIKA-AUBURN NEWS

BOTTOM RIGHT: Auburn quarterback Cameron Newton (2) is surrounded by press after the 2011 BCS National Championship Game. VASHA HUNT/OPELIKA-AUBURN NEWS

ABOVE: Auburn Head Coach Gene Chizik hoists the trophy with Auburn defensive lineman Nick Fairley (90) at his side after the 2011 BCS National Championship Game. VASHA HUNT/OPELIKA-AUBURN NEWS

ABOVE: David Gravette of Auburn rolls Toomer's Corner following the win in the BCS Championship Game. CLIFF WILLIAMS/OPELIKA-AUBURN NEWS

ABOVE LEFT: Auburn fans celebrate the win in the BCS Championship Game at 17-16 in downtown Auburn. CLIFF WILLIAMS/OPELIKA-AUBURN NEWS

LEFT: Fans braved frigid temperatures to give Toomer's Corner a monumental rolling. CLIFF WILLIAMS/OPELIKA-AUBURN NEWS

OPPOSITE: Auburn quarterback Cam Newton is overcome with emotion after winning the national championship. VASHA HUNT/OPELIKA-AUBURN NEWS

THE CHAMPION
LIVES HERE!

ABOVE: The Opelika-Auburn News had an extra edition at Toomer's Corner following a win in the BCS Championship Game. CLIFF WILLIAMS/OPELIKA-AUBURN NEWS

ABOVE RIGHT: Tiger Rags employee Daniel Stanley helps print championship shirts. CLIFF WILLIAMS/OPELIKA-AUBURN NEWS

RIGHT: Auburn fans Jennifer Wallz, left, of Opelika, Ala., and Jason Carlisle, of Alexander City, Ala., kiss to celebrate the win at Toomer's Corner. CLIFF WILLIAMS/OPELIKA-AUBURN NEWS